FREEDOM FIGHT

AS A WRIGHT FOR MANY (ALL)

DR. (Maj) C. S. RAO

INDIA • SINGAPORE • MALAYSIA

ISBN 979-8-89446-372-8

Contents

Introduction: The Prelude to Revolution

"A great man is different from an eminent one in that he is ready to be the servant of the society." – B. R. Ambedkar

In the early 1900s, India was ready for change. People wanted freedom, not just from foreign rule but from the unfair system that hurt them for so long. During World War II, when the whole world was busy fighting elsewhere, many in India were fighting their own battles for justice. These weren't always big fights with loud voices. Often, they were small acts of courage, like people gathering quietly at night to share their dreams of a free India, or spreading ideas of change without making much noise.

These small acts were very important. They were like seeds of a big movement for freedom. They showed that wanting change didn't always mean shouting it out loud. Sometimes, it was about staying strong together and believing in what's right. This book wants to tell the stories of those moments and the people who made them happen. It's about recognising their part in guiding India toward being a free country.

World War II

The premature onset of World War II and its effects on India were profound and multifaceted, impacting the country's economy, society, and its push for independence. India's participation in the war was not a matter of choice but a consequence of being part of the British Empire. Despite not being directly involved in the cause of the war, India played a crucial role by contributing significantly to the Allied war effort.

Economic and Social Impact

World War II had a significant economic impact on India, leading to widespread economic dislocation at all levels of society. India was turned into a vast logistics base for the Allies, hosting hundreds of thousands of troops from various countries. This transformation, while critical for the war effort, further strained India's resources and exacerbated the poverty that affected the majority of its population. The British war effort imposed heavy taxes on the Indian populace, compelled them to buy war bonds, and led to an inflationary spiral that severely affected the common man. The Bengal Famine of 1943-44, which resulted in the deaths of approximately 3 million Indians, highlighted the dire consequences of the British prioritising war efforts over the needs of the Indian population. This series of events eroded any remaining support for British rule among Indians.

Contributions to the War Effort

Despite the hardships, India contributed significantly to the war effort. Over 2.5 million Indian soldiers volunteered to fight for the Allies, serving with distinction in various theatres of war across the globe. These soldiers came from humble backgrounds but showed tremendous courage and determination. Their sacrifices were substantial, with over 36,000 losing their lives and many more wounded or taken as prisoners of war. The contribution of Indian soldiers was instrumental in securing victory in key battles in North Africa, Italy, and Southeast Asia. Beyond the battlefield, Indian men and women supported the war effort in various capacities, including serving in merchant ships, providing medical care, and contributing to war funds through the Indian Comforts Fund.

Impact on Indian Independence

The war expedited the process of Indian independence. The economic toll, combined with the visible proof of British vulnerability, galvanised Indian nationalist movements. The Indian National Army (INA), although its military value was limited, became a symbol of Indian resistance against British rule. The trials of INA officers, defended by future Indian leaders like Jawaharlal Nehru, and the naval mutinies of 1946, demonstrated the extent of Indian unrest and the British inability to maintain control. The post-war period saw the British acknowledging the inevitability of Indian independence, culminating in the transfer of power in 1947. This development occurred two years before the scheduled dates.

The experience of World War II was a turning point for India, It made people want independence more and showed that India is important globally. People in India did a lot during the war, and it helped end colonial rule faster.

The Russian Revolution

The Russian Revolution of 1917, led by Vladimir Lenin's Bolshevik Party, was a pivotal event that ended centuries of czarist rule in Russia and established a socialist state. This revolution resonated globally, inspiring movements for social and political justice, including in India, where it had a significant impact on the freedom struggle and political thought.

In India, the Russian Revolution inspired various segments of society, from workers and peasants to intellectuals and political leaders. The revolution's success in overthrowing an entrenched monarchy and establishing a government based on socialist principles provided a powerful example for Indian nationalists and revolutionaries grappling with British colonial rule.

Impact on Indian Workers and Farmers

The immediate aftermath of the Russian Revolution saw a surge in workers' movements in India. In 1918 and 1919, there were widespread strikes in the textile mills of Bombay, reflecting the growing consciousness among Indian workers about their rights and the potential for collective action. The establishment of the All-India Trade Union Congress in 1920 was a direct outcome of this inspired mobilisation.

Influence on Indian Political Thought

The Russian Revolution also had a profound impact on Indian political thought. Leaders like Jawaharlal Nehru acknowledged the Soviet Revolution as a significant leap forward for human society, laying the foundation for a new civilisation. The promise of socialism influenced the formation of a Congress Socialist group within the Indian National Congress in 1930, reflecting the growing interest in Marxist and socialist ideas among Indian nationalists.

Revolutionary Activities Inspired by Russian Methods

Indian revolutionaries, inspired by the events in Russia, adopted more assertive tactics against British rule. Newspapers and publications advocated revolutionary activities, drawing parallels between the struggles in Russia and India, and highlighting the effectiveness of direct action and armed struggle. This period saw a rise in revolutionary acts, including bombings and assassinations aimed at British officials, inspired by the Russian example.

Gandhi and Lenin: Divergent Paths with Mutual Respect

Despite their differing approaches to achieving political goals, with Gandhi advocating non-violence and Lenin leading a violent revolution, there was mutual respect between the ideologies they represented. Both leaders were seen as guiding forces for their respective countries' struggles against oppression, and their efforts demonstrated that profound changes in society are possible through both peaceful and revolutionary means. India's first Prime Minister, Jawaharlal Nehru, noted the influence of Lenin's revolution on India's freedom movement, despite Gandhi's nonviolent approach.

As we turn the page from this global backdrop to focus on India's soil, we start on the journey from dark to light with the Bhīma Koregam Martyrs Day—A powerful reminder of the sacrifices and firm spirit of those who bravely dreamed of freedom despite impossible challenges. This book honours their memory and lights the path they showed for the generations that followed, setting the foundation for a nation's unstoppable pursuit of liberty and equality.

"Ambedkar's Journey for Equality"

Dr. B.R. Ambedkar's life was a remarkable journey of self-education and relentless struggle for equality. Born into a caste that was considered untouchable, he faced discrimination and social exclusion from a young age. Despite these challenges, Ambedkar's determination to improve his and others' situations drove him to pursue higher education, a rare achievement for someone from his background at that time and applicable till date.

Ambedkar went on to study in some of the most prestigious universities in the world, including Columbia University in the United States and the London School of Economics in the UK. These experiences broadened his perspective on social injustices and equipped him with the knowledge to challenge them. He became a leading intellectual in India, advocating for the rights of the marginalised and oppressed.

In India, society was sharply divided into two broad groups based on wealth, power, and social status. The first group, comprised of the wealthy and powerful, had access to quality education and significant influence in societal affairs. They benefited from maintaining the status quo, which kept them in positions of authority and comfort. This group often resisted changes that could disrupt their privileged standing, preferring to keep the existing power structures intact.

The second group, on the other hand, consisted of individuals from less privileged backgrounds. This included a vast majority who lived in poverty, lacked access to basic education, and had little to no representation in the political and social spheres. Despite their hard work and contributions to society, they remained marginalised and were often denied the rights and opportunities afforded to the more affluent class. This systemic inequality led to a lack of empowerment among these individuals, many of whom accepted their circumstances without the means or support to challenge them.

Dr. B.R. Ambedkar dedicated his life to advocating for the rights of the marginalised. Coming from a background of oppression himself, he understood the deep-seated injustices that plagued Indian society. He used his education and intellect to fight against these injustices, aiming to uplift those who were systematically denied equality and dignity.

Ambedkar's efforts included a wide range of activities aimed at challenging and changing the prevailing inequalities. He was a prolific writer, and his books and essays critically examined the social and economic barriers that perpetuated inequality. Through his speeches, he reached out to the masses, inspiring them to aspire to a more equitable society.

Moreover, Ambedkar played a pivotal role in shaping India's legal and constitutional framework. As the chairman of the drafting committee for the Indian Constitution, he ensured that the principles of justice, liberty, equality, and fraternity were enshrined as the cornerstones of the nation. He advocated for affirmative action, including reservation of seats in education, legislative assemblies and government jobs, to improve the socioeconomic status of the marginalised communities.

Ambedkar's legacy shows he believed in a society where everyone, no matter their background, can have the same chance to do well. His life and work continue to inspire efforts toward achieving social justice and equality in India and around the world.

Indian independence movement brought in great thoughts which are highlighted to give in some time and understand the contribution done to the betterment of human race, it is the great leadership Skill, intellectual might and undisputed love of Dr B R Ambedkar for co-humans which is reflected through subtopic in this book. Hoping this small literature will trigger new thoughts for better Indian with better quality Indians

CHAPTER 1

From Dark to Light - Bhīma Koragam Martyrs Day

The Battle of Bhima Koregaon was not just a military confrontation but a pivotal moment that reflected the complex interplay of colonial power dynamics, military strategy, and social hierarchies in 19th-century India. This battle was a demonstration of the broader Third Anglo-Maratha War, which was instrumental in establishing British dominance over the Indian subcontinent. It marked the decline of Maratha power, paving the way for nearly two centuries of British rule.

Why the Battle Started

The immediate cause of the battle was the British East India Company's efforts to assert its dominance over the Indian subcontinent. By the early 19th century, the British were in direct conflict with the Maratha Confederacy, one of the last major indigenous powers that resisted British control. The Third Anglo-Maratha War, of which the Battle of Bhima Koregaon was a part, was a decisive conflict that led to the collapse of Maratha power and the consolidation of British rule in India.

The Maratha Confederacy, once a formidable power that challenged the Mughal Empire and even the British, was weakened by internal strife and succession disputes. The Peshwa, the prime minister and de facto leader of the Maratha Confederacy, sought to reclaim lost authority and territory but faced significant challenges from the British, who were keen on expanding their territories and securing their interests in the region.

The Need for the Battle

From a strategic standpoint, the British needed to defeat the Maratha forces to secure their position in India. The Battle of Bhima Koregaon was critical in this regard because it demonstrated the military prowess and resolve of the British forces against a numerically superior enemy. A victory would not only demoralise the Maratha forces but also send a strong message to other Indian states about the futility of resisting British power.

For the Marathas, resisting British advances was crucial to maintaining their sovereignty and protecting their way of life. The Marathas, under Peshwa Baji Rao II, were fighting to preserve their dominion from being annexed by the British. However, the fragmentation within the Maratha Confederacy and the superior military tactics of the British eventually led to their downfall.

The Origin

In the time leading up to the Battle of Bhima Koregaon, there were two main sides. On one side was the British regiment, which was not very large, having around 800 people. These included the leaders and soldiers, known as officers, JCOs (Junior Commissioned Officers), and NCOs (Non-Commissioned Officers or men). Facing them was the army of the Peshwa king, which was much larger, with a total of 28,000 men and officers.

Seeing how outnumbered they were, the British officers started thinking about leaving, not sure if they could win against such a large number. But then, something interesting happened. The Peshwa king tried to secretly convince the Indian soldiers who were with the British to come and join his side instead.

Among the British regiment were about 500 soldiers from the Mahar community, along with a few others from different communities in India. These Mahar soldiers wanted to be treated with respect and as equals by the Peshwa king, but he refused. This refusal didn't stop the Mahar soldiers. Instead, they went to the British officers, talked with them, and got permission to fight under the British flag against the Peshwa's much bigger army.

This decision led to a remarkable moment: just 500 men stood ready to face off against 28,000. It's reminiscent of the epic Battle of Waterloo fought by Napoleon, but here, the fight was for their dignity and right to be recognised as humans deserving of respect. This bravery and the stand they took are remembered to this day, with the names of those who died or were injured being honored on a war memorial.

This background sets the stage for understanding the depth of courage and the strong desire for respect that drove the Mahar soldiers to take part in this battle. It wasn't just a military conflict; it was a stand for dignity and recognition in the face of overwhelming odds.

The Significance Of The Battle

The Battle of Bhima Koregaon, fought on January 1, 1818, between the British East India Company and the Peshwa faction of the Maratha Confederacy, holds immense significance for Dalits, particularly the Mahar community. This battle is celebrated as a momentous victory over caste oppression, as it featured a significant participation from the Dalit Mahars, who were part of the British forces. Despite being outnumbered, with 500 Mahars among the 800 troops of the British army facing a 28,000-strong Peshwa force, the British and their Mahar soldiers managed to fend off the Peshwa's attack, leading to a historic victory that is seen as a symbol of Dalit valour and resistance against high-caste Brahmin oppression.

The Peshwas, who were Brahmins, are known to have ill-treated the Dalits in the region, perpetuating a system of caste-based discrimination and social exclusion. The victory of the Mahars and other Dalits alongside the British is thus celebrated for challenging this social order and asserting the strength and valour of the oppressed against their oppressors. The Mahar soldiers, who fought valiantly in the battle, were commemorated with a victory pillar in Koregaon, which carries the names of 22 Mahar soldiers seriously injured among with the 49 who died fighting for the East India Company.

The significance of the Battle of Bhima Koregaon extends beyond its immediate military outcome. It symbolises a critical challenge to the caste-based discrimination endemic in Indian society and offers a counter-narrative to stories of caste and social dominance. Dr. B.R. Ambedkar's visit to the site on January 1, 1927, further cemented its importance in Dalit history, making it a rallying point for Dalit pride and resistance against casteism. Every year, thousands of Dalits visit the victory pillar to pay homage to the valour of their forefathers, turning it into a symbol of Dalit pride and resistance against caste oppression.

The Battle of Bhima Koregaon and its commemoration highlight the ongoing struggle for dignity, equality, and social justice in the face of enduring casteism. It serves as a reminder of the potential for change and the nobility of the fight against oppression, inspiring future generations to continue striving for a more equitable society.

Global Context and Parallels

American War of Independence

The Boston Tea Party was a significant event in American history, taking place on the night of December 16, 1773. It was a protest by the American colonists against the British government and the monopolistic East India Company that controlled all the tea imported into the colonies. At the heart of the protest were issues of "no taxation without representation," as the British government had imposed taxes on tea and other goods without giving the colonies a voice in the British Parliament.

Colonists, led by the Sons of Liberty, a group of patriots who sought to oppose British policies, dressed as Mohawk Indians to disguise their identities. They boarded three ships docked in Boston Harbour—the Dartmouth, the Eleanor, and the Beaver—that were laden with tea. In a defiant act of resistance, they threw 342 chests of tea, worth an estimated £9,000 (a significant sum at the time), into the harbour waters. This act was meant to send a clear message to Britain about the colonists' refusal to comply with the Tea Act, which they believed was unjust.

When we look at these two pivotal moments in history, the Boston Tea Party and the Battle of Bhima Koregaon, we see a common thread of resistance against unjust authority. The Boston Tea Party, a protest against unfair British taxes and monopolistic practices, happened when American colonists, feeling the heavy hand of British economic control without any say in the matter, decided to take a stand. They disguised themselves and threw a large amount of tea into Boston Harbour on December 16, 1773. This bold move was their way of saying "no" to the British government's unfair taxes and control over the tea trade.

Just like the Boston Tea Party was more than just about tea, the Battle of Bhima Koregaon was more than just a military conflict. It represented a stand against the deep-rooted caste discrimination in Indian society. The Mahar soldiers, fighting alongside the British, challenged the existing social hierarchies dominated by the upper castes. Their triumph was a powerful symbol of resistance against oppression and a source of hope for those facing adversity.

After the Boston Tea Party, the British government enforced tough rules called the Intolerable Acts to control the colonies. Instead of stopping independence, these acts brought the colonies together, leading to the

American Revolutionary War. This shows that oppressed people may unite to fight for freedom and justice.

Both these historical events, though set in different continents and times, underline a universal truth: the desire for dignity, representation, and justice can drive people to remarkable acts of defiance. The colonists' and the Mahar soldiers' struggles remind us that standing up against unfair systems is a powerful step toward change. These moments of defiance against unjust authority not only shaped the course of history in their respective nations but also continued to inspire the fight for equality and justice around the world.

The French Revolution

The French Revolution, spanning from 1789 to 1799, was a period of radical social and political upheaval in France that had a lasting impact on French history and the broader course of world events. Its inception marked the decline of monarchies and churches social power in Europe, laying the groundwork for the rise of democracy and secular societies.

Causes

The revolution's roots can be traced to a confluence of social, economic, and political factors. A rigid social structure divided society into three estates: the clergy (First Estate), the nobility (Second Estate), and the common people (Third Estate), with the latter bearing the brunt of high taxes and economic hardship. The financial crisis, exacerbated by France's involvement in expensive wars, including support for the American Revolution, left the French monarchy in a precarious financial situation. King Louis XVI's attempts to solve the crisis through taxation reform met with resistance from the privileged estates and led to widespread discontent.

Its core principles of Liberty, Equality, and Fraternity were not just ideological slogans but were deeply integrated into the fabric of the new society it aimed to create. These principles resonate closely with the aspirations of the Bhima Koregaon warriors, symbolising a universal struggle for dignity, rights, and unity against oppression.

Liberty in the French Revolution signified the profound desire of the people to free themselves from the oppressive structures of absolute monarchy and aristocratic privilege. This mirrors the aspirations of the Mahar soldiers at Bhima Koregaon, who fought for their freedom and dignity against a backdrop of caste-based discrimination and social exclusion.

Equality was another foundational pillar of the French Revolution, aiming to dismantle the deeply entrenched hierarchies and privileges of the feudal system. This pursuit of a more equitable society parallels the struggle of the Bhima Koregaon warriors against the rigid caste hierarchies that marginalised and oppressed the Dalits for centuries.

Fraternity, though sometimes less emphasised, was critical in the French Revolution for fostering a sense of collective identity and unity among the citizens of France, transcending regional, class, and religious divisions. Similarly, the Battle of Bhima Koregaon is celebrated by Dalits as a symbol of their collective strength and unity in the face of systemic oppression.

The storming of the Bastille and ending special privileges, setting up the National Assembly, and writing the Rights of Man and Citizen were important parts of the French Revolution. They showed a dedication to freedom, equality, and brotherhood.

Russian Revolution

The Bolshevik Revolution, also known as the October Revolution of 1917, fundamentally transformed Russia from a monarchy under Tsar Nicholas II to a socialist state under the leadership of the Bolshevik Party, led by Vladimir Lenin. It was the second phase of the Russian Revolution, following the February Revolution, which had overthrown the Tsarist autocracy but failed to establish a stable government. The Bolsheviks seized this opportunity to advocate for a radical restructuring of society based on Marxist principles, emphasising the abolition of class hierarchies, the distribution of wealth, and the dignity of every individual, regardless of their social status.

Emphasis on the Dignity of Every Life

The Bolshevik Revolution was underpinned by the Marxist belief in the inherent value and dignity of every life, opposing the exploitation and dehumanisation of workers under capitalism. It aimed to create a classless society where resources and power were equitably shared, ensuring that every individual's needs were met. This vision resonated deeply in a country plagued by poverty, inequality, and imperialist wars that had caused immense suffering for the Russian peasantry and working class.

Inspirational Value for Indian Freedom Fighters and Social Reformers

The Bolshevik Revolution held significant inspirational value for Indian freedom fighters and social reformers, many of whom were grappling with similar issues of colonial exploitation, social inequality, and the struggle for self-determination. The revolution's success demonstrated the power of mass mobilisation and the potential to overthrow entrenched systems of oppression, providing a model of revolutionary change that influenced various movements across the globe.

Prominent Indian nationalists, including Jawaharlal Nehru and Subhas Chandra Bose, were inspired by the Soviet model of development and its emphasis on planning, industrialisation, and social welfare. Nehru, in particular, admired the Soviet Union's rapid transformation into an industrial power and its efforts to eradicate poverty and illiteracy.

The revolution's focus on equality and justice also inspired social reformers in India, who were fighting against the caste system and advocating for the rights of the marginalised. The Bolsheviks' commitment to ending discrimination and promoting social inclusion offered a compelling vision for a more equitable society.

The Bolshevik Revolution was a big moment in Russian history and gave hope to oppressed people everywhere. It focused on valuing every life and making big changes, which motivated Indian freedom fighters and social reformers to aim for a fairer society. Even though people argue about how the Soviet state turned out, the original ideas of the revolution still inspire those fighting against unfairness and inequality.

The Battle

The Battle of Bhima Koregaon and the subsequent commemoration of the event hold deep symbolic importance within the Dalit community and the broader Indian society, signifying resistance, valour, and the quest for dignity against oppressive caste structures.

Martyrdom and Symbolic Importance

Symbol of Resistance: The Mahar soldiers' participation and valour in the Battle of Bhima Koregaon are seen as a powerful act of resistance against the caste oppression perpetuated by the Peshwa regime. Their ability to stand up to a much larger and dominant force is celebrated as a moment of defiance and assertion of dignity by the marginalised.

Commemoration as a Rallying Point: The annual gathering at the Bhima Koregaon memorial, especially after Dr. B.R. Ambedkar's visit in 1927, has turned the site into a symbolic rallying point for the Dalit community. It serves as a reminder of their historical struggles and achievements, and of the ongoing fight against caste discrimination and social inequality.

Inspiration for Social Reform: The narrative of Bhima Koregaon extends beyond the Dalit community to inspire broader movements for social justice and reform in India. It underscores the importance of confronting social injustices and highlights the potential for marginalised groups to challenge and change oppressive systems.

Unity and Solidarity: The commemoration of the battle has become an occasion for fostering unity and solidarity among Dalits and between them and other oppressed communities. It is a manifestation of collective memory that strengthens community bonds and reaffirms a shared commitment to equality and justice.

Reinterpretation and Relevance: Over the years, the symbolism of Bhima Koregaon has been reinterpreted and recontextualized in light of contemporary struggles against casteism and social justice. It stands as a testament to the enduring relevance of the battle in the fight for dignity and rights for the oppressed.

Educational Impact: The story of Bhima Koregaon also serves an educational purpose, highlighting the contributions of Dalits to India's history that have often been overlooked or marginalised in mainstream narratives. It promotes a more inclusive understanding of Indian history that acknowledges the diversity of experiences and struggles within the nation.

Role In Contemporary Social And Political Movements

The memorialisation of the Battle of Bhima Koregaon has evolved significantly over time, becoming a potent symbol in contemporary social and political movements in India. This process of memorialisation has not only preserved the memory of the battle but has also served as a platform for advocating social justice, equality, and resistance against oppression.

The centrepiece of this memorialisation is the victory pillar (obelisk) erected at the site of the battle in Koregaon Bhima. Inscribed with the names of the soldiers who fought in the battle, the pillar stands as a testament to their bravery and the sacrifices made. It has become a place of pilgrimage for the Dalit community, symbolising their struggle for dignity and rights.

Dr. B.R. Ambedkar's visit to the site on January 1, 1927, played a crucial role in transforming the memorial into a rallying point for the Dalit movement. His homage to the fallen soldiers was a profound act of reclaiming history and affirming the Dalit community's role in the nation's past. Since then, January 1st has been commemorated annually at Bhima Koregaon, drawing thousands of people from across the country to pay their respects and celebrate the ideals of equality and justice.

The commemoration of Bhima Koregaon has increasingly become intertwined with contemporary social and political movements, serving as a symbol of resistance against caste-based discrimination and social inequality. It embodies the struggle for a more equitable society, inspiring activists and social reformers to continue the fight against oppression.

1. **Dalit Rights and Social Justice:** The annual gatherings at Bhima Koregaon have become a platform for articulating demands for Dalit rights and broader social justice issues. They highlight ongoing challenges faced by marginalised communities and call for action to address discrimination, violence, and inequality.

2. **Unity Against Oppression:** The memorialisation of Bhima Koregaon has fostered unity among Dalits and other marginalised groups, building solidarity in the face of oppressive structures. It underscores the importance of collective action and the strength derived from shared struggles.

3. **Political Significance:** Bhima Koregaon has also gained political significance, with various political parties and leaders participating in the commemoration events. It reflects the

battle's role in shaping political discourse around caste, identity, and social justice in India.

4. **Cultural and Educational Impact:** Through art, literature, and academic work, Bhima Koregaon has been explored and presented in ways that educate and sensitise the broader public about Dalit history and contributions. This cultural engagement has played a key role in challenging stereotypes and fostering a more inclusive understanding of Indian history.

5. **International Recognition:** The narrative of Bhima Koregaon has transcended national boundaries, receiving attention and solidarity from international human rights organisations and diaspora communities. This global dimension emphasises the universal struggle against discrimination and injustice.

Sound of Freedom

The Battle of Bhima Koregaon, fought over two centuries ago, continues to resonate in contemporary India, particularly in the context of social justice and equality movements. Its relevance today can be seen through various lenses, including its role in inspiring movements for caste equity, influencing political discourse, and shaping collective memory and identity.

Inspiration for Movements for Caste Equity

The Battle of Bhima Koregaon is a symbol of fighting against caste discrimination in India. It inspires ongoing efforts for fair treatment and equal rights for all. Activists use its legacy to support policies that promote equality and social inclusion.

Influence on Political Discourse

The battle's commemoration events have become platforms for addressing contemporary issues related to caste, discrimination, and social inequality. Political leaders and parties, recognising the symbolic power of Bhima Koregaon, often engage with commemorations to signal their commitment to social justice and appeal to marginalised constituencies. This engagement highlights the battle's role in influencing political discourse and public policy related to social equity.

Shaping Collective Memory and Identity

The annual commemorations of Bhima Koregaon play a crucial role in shaping the collective memory and identity of the Dalit community for Indians. These events not only serve to remember the past but also to affirm the community's contributions to India's history and to assert their rights and dignity in the present. By celebrating the valour of the Mahar soldiers, the Dalit community challenges historical narratives that have marginalised their contributions and foster a sense of pride and belonging.

Educating and Raising Awareness in Society

The story of Bhima Koregaon is increasingly being incorporated into educational curricula, literature, and public discourse, helping to educate and sensitize broader society about the complexities of caste and the importance of social justice. Through films, books, and academic research, the battle's significance is being explored and presented in ways that challenge stereotypes and promote a more inclusive understanding of Indian society.

Global Solidarity

The relevance of Bhima Koregaon extends beyond India's borders, with international human rights organizations and diaspora communities recognizing and supporting the battle's commemorative events. This global dimension underscores the universal struggle against oppression and discrimination, fostering solidarity and support for social justice movements around the world.

Martyrs' Day

The Battle of Bhima Koregaon plays a crucial role in empowering marginalized communities, especially the Dalit community, by highlighting a moment in history where they showcased valor against oppression. The annual commemoration of this event serves as an important occasion to reinforce unity and resilience among these communities.

Empowering Marginalised Communities

Acknowledgment of Historical Valor: Recognizing the bravery of the Mahar soldiers in the battle against a much larger force challenges historical narratives that have often marginalized certain communities. It provides a narrative of strength and courage that contrasts with depictions of victimhood.

Building Community Pride: The celebration of this event helps in building a sense of pride among the Dalit community. It's a reminder of their contributions to history and a tool for strengthening community identity.

Motivation for Action: The story of the battle serves as motivation for current and future generations to continue advocating for their rights and striving for a society that values equality and justice.

Significance of Annual Commemoration

Unity Among Communities: The gathering of thousands of people from various backgrounds for the commemoration highlights unity among oppressed communities. It shows a collective stand against discrimination and social injustice.

Platform for Discussion: The commemoration provides a platform to discuss the ongoing challenges faced by marginalized communities, including caste-based violence and discrimination. It's an opportunity to voice concerns and call for change.

Drive for Social Change: Beyond remembering the past, the event also acts as a driving force for social and political movements aimed at achieving rights for marginalized groups. It's about making a positive impact on the future.

Conclusion

In this chapter, we've looked at how people, facing tough challenges due to unfairness and discrimination, managed to change their situation for the better. It's a story about moving from hard times, filled with struggle and injustice, to better days where there's more fairness and respect for everyone.

Think of it this way: people were in a tough spot, like being in a dark room with no windows. But they didn't give up. Instead, they found small cracks where light could come in. Over time, those cracks got bigger until the room was filled with light. Events like the Battle of Bhima Koregaon are examples of those moments when the light started to come in, showing that when people work together and stand up for what's right, they can make a big difference.

The story doesn't end there, though. Every year, when people remember these events and keep working for what's fair, it's like they're making sure the light stays on. They're making sure that the progress made isn't forgotten, and that there's always a push toward making things even better.

So, this chapter isn't just looking back at what happened. It's also about seeing how far we've come and reminding us that there's still work to do. It tells us that no matter how hard things might seem, there's always a way to make them better, step by step.

CHAPTER 2

Voices Unheard - Representation to Simon Commission

The Prelude to Representation

The Government of India Act of 1919, also known as the Montagu-Chelmsford Reforms, marked a significant step in the British administration's approach to governing India. It was established to gradually increase the participation of Indians in governance, introducing a dual system of government known as "dyarchy" at the provincial level. This system divided the administration into two categories: transferred and reserved subjects. Transferred subjects, such as education and health, were to be administered by Indian ministers responsible to the legislative councils, while reserved subjects like law and order remained under British control. The Act also expanded the legislative councils and introduced some form of electoral representation for Indians, albeit with a limited franchise based on property, tax, or education qualifications.

Despite these reforms, the Act faced criticism for not going far enough in granting self-governance and for maintaining significant control over financial and legislative processes in the hands of the British. The central legislature was bicameral but had limited powers, with the Governor-General retaining the right to veto bills, issue ordinances, and enact laws without legislative consent if deemed necessary for the country's peace. The Act's introduction of dyarchy was seen as complicated and ineffective, leading to friction between elected Indian ministers and the British-appointed executive councillors who were not responsible to the legislature.

The reaction in India was mixed. While some leaders accepted the Act and cooperated with the government, the Indian National Congress and other nationalist figures found it disappointing and unsatisfactory, advocating instead for full self-government. Prominent leaders like Bal Gangadhar Tilak and M.K. Gandhi publicly criticised the reforms, with Tilak calling it "a sunless dawn" and Gandhi remarking on its inadequacy for truly addressing India's need for autonomy.

The 1920s and 1930s in India were a period marked by significant political and social upheaval, with the Communist Party of India (CPI) emerging as a notable force within the national movement. Founded on 26 December 1925 in Kanpur, the CPI aimed to unite various communist groups under one umbrella, despite facing severe restrictions and surveillance by British colonial authorities. The party's growth was hampered by legal prohibitions and criminal prosecutions, leading to its operations being conducted in secrecy and through indirect means such as the Workers and Peasants Parties.

The involvement of communist ideology in the Indian independence movement also saw direct actions, such as the protest against the Simon Commission, which culminated in the bombing of the Central Legislative Assembly in Delhi as a demonstration against repressive laws. This period also witnessed the formation of revolutionary groups within prisons, such as the Communist Consolidation in 1935, which led to hunger strikes demanding political prisoner status and better treatment, showing the resilience and dedication of communists toward their cause.

Jawaharlal Nehru's advocacy for socialism significantly shaped the Indian National Congress's direction, bringing the ideas of class struggle and economic equality to the forefront of the national movement. Despite differing views with Mahatma Gandhi on economic and social policies, Nehru saw the importance of integrating socialist principles with the broader struggle for independence, aiming to transform Congress into a more inclusive and radical movement that could address the needs of the working class and peasants.

The period also saw active engagement with the Soviet Union, with Indian revolutionaries being influenced by the Bolshevik revolution. Figures like M.N. Roy played a critical role in this exchange, founding the CPI in Tashkent with Lenin's encouragement and advocating for a unified front against colonialism while pushing for socialist reforms within India.

The Simon Commission, officially named the Indian Statutory Commission, was established by the British Government in 1927. Its primary purpose was to review the workings of the Government of India Act 1919, also known as the Montagu-Chelmsford Reforms, and to propose further reforms. The commission was led by Sir John Simon, with all its members being British officials, which immediately sparked controversy and led to widespread opposition in India.

The exclusion of Indian members from the commission was a significant point of contention, as it was seen as a deliberate attempt to sideline Indians from discussing their country's future. This move was perceived as a clear indication of the British government's unwillingness to genuinely consider Indian aspirations for greater self-governance. In response, major political parties and leaders across India, including the Indian National Congress and the Muslim League, decided to boycott the commission.

The commission's arrival in India in 1927 was met with massive protests under the slogan "Simon Go Back." These protests were widespread and included demonstrations, strikes, and hartals (shutdowns), showcasing a united front against the commission. The protests were not limited to any one region but occurred across the country, from Bombay (now Mumbai) to Lahore, highlighting the pan-Indian opposition to the commission. The most notable incident of protest against the Simon Commission was in Lahore, where a peaceful demonstration led by Lala Lajpat Rai was violently dispersed by the police, resulting in Rai's death from his injuries.

The Indian response to the Simon Commission had profound implications. It brought together various strands of the Indian independence movement, demonstrating the capacity for coordinated action against colonial rule. The widespread opposition to the commission also underlined the Indian people's increasing discontent with British policies and their desire for true self-governance. This opposition was a clear signal to the British that any further reforms that did not include substantial moves towards self-rule would not be accepted.

In the aftermath, the British government's acknowledgment of the commission's failure led to the Round Table Conferences, which sought to find a new approach to Indian constitutional reform. However, the legacy of the Simon Commission's visit remained a testament to the growing nationalist sentiment in India and the unifying cause it provided for Indians from diverse political and social backgrounds.

The Communication Breakdown

The British Raj's governance of India, from its establishment in 1858 following the Indian Mutiny to the partition and independence in 1947, was characterised by a series of administrative reforms aimed at increasing Indian participation in governance. However, these reforms often fell short of Indian aspirations for self-rule, leading to an adamant national independence movement that grew particularly strong in the 20th century.

By the 1920s and 1930s, the Indian National Congress, along with other political entities, was vigorously campaigning for independence, utilizing strategies of non-cooperation and civil disobedience to pressure the British government. Despite some Muslim leaders' initial hopes for a unified Indian federation, the concept of a separate state for Muslims gained traction, particularly with the All-India Muslim League under the leadership of Mohammed Ali Jinnah.

The British government's decision to partition India into two independent dominions, India and Pakistan, was largely influenced by the escalating Hindu-Muslim tensions and the violent communal clashes that erupted, notably the "Great Calcutta Killing" of 1946. These events demonstrated the deep divisions within Indian society and underscored the challenges of creating a unified independent state that could accommodate the diverse religious and cultural identities within India.

Lord Mountbatten's arrival in India in 1947 as the last Viceroy was crucial in hastening the process towards independence and partition. Convinced that swift and decisive action was necessary to prevent further bloodshed and chaos, Mountbatten proposed the partition plan, which was rapidly implemented, leading to the independence of India and Pakistan in August 1947. This decision was met with massive population displacements and communal violence, highlighting the complexities and challenges of ending colonial rule and establishing independent states.

Communication in governance, particularly in the context of the British Raj in India, experienced significant failures that contributed to the growing discontent and ultimately the push for independence. The period of British rule, or the British Raj, extended from 1858 to 1947, following the Indian Rebellion of 1857. This era was marked by a series of reforms intended to increase Indian participation in governance, yet the powerlessness of Indians to determine their own future without the consent of the British led to an increasingly adamant national independence movement.

The governance failures of the East India Company, particularly its insensitivity towards Indian religions and its oppressive rule, led to the Sepoy Mutiny of 1857. This mutiny underscored the communication breakdown between the rulers and the ruled, as it was partly incited by rumors that new rifle cartridges were greased with fat from pigs and cows, which was offensive to Muslim and Hindu soldiers respectively. The violent suppression of this revolt and the subsequent transfer of power from the East India Company to the British Crown did little to address the root issues of miscommunication and disregard for Indian sentiments.

Under the British Raj, efforts to increase Indian participation in governance, such as the introduction of the Indian Legislative Council with an Indian-nominated element in 1861, were seen as too little and too late. These reforms often appeared as mere tokenism rather than genuine attempts to integrate Indian voices into the governance process. The policy of consultation with Indians, initiated after the mutiny to prevent similar crises, was perceived as insufficient and highlighted the British administration's failure to genuinely understand and address Indian aspirations.

Moreover, the structure of governance under the Raj, with its imperial political structure and centralised power in the hands of the British Crown and the Viceroy, further alienated Indians. Despite the nominal inclusion of Indian languages and the appointment of Indians to certain legislative positions, the overarching control remained with British officials, and significant decisions regarding India's future were made without adequate Indian consultation.

This communication breakdown in governance, characterized by British insensitivity to Indian cultural and political aspirations, and the failure to effectively integrate Indian perspectives into the governance process, fuelled discontent. It highlighted the inherent issues in colonial governance models, where the colonized were seen as subjects rather than equal stakeholders in their administration. The eventual push for independence was as much a rejection of British rule as it was a demand for self-governance where communication and representation were central.

Raising the Question of Inequality

During the era of the British Raj in India, the imposition of British laws and social norms significantly impacted marginalized communities, leading to profound and long-lasting inequalities and injustices. One notable instance was the criminalization of homosexuality, which was a direct result of British colonial laws. This legislation was alien to Indian society, where diverse sexual orientations had historically been more accepted. The British imposition of Victorian morality not only marginalized the LGBTQ+ community but also entrenched homophobia and sexism within Indian society, effects that persist to this day.

The British Raj also deepened economic disparities and exploited India's resources, exacerbating conditions for the rural poor and contributing to widespread famines and poverty. Between 1880 and 1920, policies and practices under British rule are estimated to have resulted in approximately 100 million deaths. This period was marked by severe famines exacerbated by British economic policies, such as the emphasis on cash crops for export over local food production, and the oppressive Zamindari system, which levied heavy taxes and rents on peasants, which led to dispossession and extreme poverty.

Economic historian Robert Allen has pointed out that the level of extreme poverty in India saw a significant increase during British rule, suggesting that living standards in India before colonialism could have been comparable to those in developing parts of Western Europe. This contradicts the often rosier picture of colonial impacts painted by some historical narratives. The introduction of the Zamindari system and the focus on cash crops for the benefit of British economic interests rather than local food security had devastating effects on India's rural population, making them vulnerable to exploitation and economic shocks.

These policies not only led to immediate suffering and loss of life but also set the stage for long-term socio-economic challenges that India has continued to grapple with post-independence. The lasting impacts of these colonial policies underscore the complex legacy of the British Raj in India, highlighting the need for continued efforts to address these historical injustices and their present-day consequences.

The Commission, officially known as the Indian Statutory Commission, was tasked with reviewing the political situation in India and suggesting constitutional reforms. However, its all-British composition led to widespread protests across India, as it was seen as another example of colonial disregard for Indian opinion.

Amidst this backdrop, various Indian leaders and communities saw the Commission's investigations as a strategic moment to raise awareness about the inequalities and injustices they faced under British rule. For marginalized communities, including the rural poor, Dalits (then referred to as "Untouchables"), and other socially and economically disadvantaged groups, the Simon Commission became a platform to articulate their demands for more equitable treatment and representation within the colonial governance structure.

Leaders like Dr. B.R. Ambedkar, who championed the cause of the Dalits, used the occasion to highlight the severe social discrimination and economic hardships faced by these communities. They argued for the need to abolish the Zamindari system, which had led to widespread exploitation of peasants, and for the introduction of measures to improve education and employment opportunities for disadvantaged groups. Furthermore, the push for the representation of marginalized communities in any new constitutional arrangement proposed by the Commission was a key demand.

This strategic move to engage with the Simon Commission, despite its widespread boycott by major political parties like the Indian National Congress, underscored a critical aspect of the Indian freedom struggle. It highlighted the diversity of voices within the movement and the complex interplay of demands for national independence alongside calls for social justice and equality.

The efforts to represent the concerns of marginalised communities to the Simon Commission can be seen as an early form of political mobilisation that would later influence post-independence India's constitutional and legal frameworks. The legacy of these strategic engagements is evident in the provisions for social justice enshrined in the Indian Constitution, including affirmative action policies and protections for disadvantaged groups.

While the Simon Commission itself did not lead to immediate reforms addressing these concerns, the articulation of demands for social justice during this period laid the groundwork for future legislative and constitutional measures in independent India.

Dr. Ambedkar's Representation

Dr. Ambedkar's contributions to the Simon Commission were significant in highlighting the injustices faced by the "depressed classes," a term he used synonymously with "untouchables." He provided detailed statistics to argue for the proper representation and treatment of these communities, emphasizing the need for a broader definition that could include various marginalized groups beyond the narrow confines of caste. Ambedkar's engagement with the Simon Commission was a part of his broader efforts to combat untouchability and promote social reform, marked by actions like the satyagraha at Mahad for water rights and the burning of the Manusmriti, a text he criticized for justifying caste discrimination.

Ambedkar was appointed to the Bombay Presidency Committee to work with the all-European Simon Commission in 1928, amidst widespread protests in India against the commission. While most Indians ignored the commission's report, Ambedkar wrote a separate set of recommendations for future constitutional reforms, highlighting his commitment to addressing the systemic inequalities of the caste system and advocating for a political identity for untouchables separate from both the Indian National Congress and British colonial authorities.

Dr. B.R. Ambedkar's role in the Indian freedom struggle and the fight for social justice is both profound and multifaceted. Known affectionately as Baba Saheb, Ambedkar's contributions extend beyond his pivotal role in drafting the Indian Constitution; he was a crusader for the rights of the marginalized and an advocate for a society based on the principles of liberty, equality, and fraternity.

Ambedkar's deep-seated opposition to the caste system and his advocacy for the rights of the "depressed classes" were central to his vision of social justice. He believed that the caste system, along with communalism, patriarchy, and the exploitation of workers, created entrenched inequalities that hindered the development of a just society. His seminal work, Annihilation of Caste, critiques the caste system's restrictions on individual freedoms and its violation of principles of equality and fraternity.

In the broader context of the Indian freedom struggle, Ambedkar's contributions were significant yet distinct from the mainstream nationalist movement led by the Indian National Congress and figures like Mahatma Gandhi. Ambedkar's advocacy for the rights of Dalits and his insistence on social justice as a precondition for true freedom placed him at odds with other leaders at times. His negotiations with Gandhi leading to the Poona Pact, which secured reserved seats for Dalits in the legislative assemblies, marked a pivotal moment in his struggle for the Dalits' rights.

As Independent India's first Law Minister, Ambedkar's legacy is indelibly linked to the Indian Constitution, which lays the foundation for a democratic India committed to justice, liberty, equality, and fraternity. He was instrumental in the Constitution Drafting Committee, facing and overcoming criticism with skill, tact, and authority. His speeches during the debates are remembered for their clarity, vision, and the balance he sought to strike between central authority and states' rights. He emphasized the dangers of hero worship in politics, advocating for a vigilant, informed, and participative citizenry.

Ambedkar's foresight and contributions to women's rights, and labor rights, and his fight against social discrimination underscore his comprehensive approach to achieving social justice. His work toward the Hindu Code Bill, although met with significant resistance, aimed at revolutionizing Hindu family law to provide equal rights to women, among other progressive reforms.

Reconciliation Committee in South Africa

After Nelson Mandela was elected as President of South Africa, the Truth and Reconciliation Commission (TRC) was established by the new government in 1995. The TRC was a court-like body created to uncover the truth about human rights violations that occurred during the period of apartheid. Its focus was on gathering evidence and uncovering information from both victims and perpetrators, rather than prosecuting individuals for past crimes, which set it apart from other post-conflict judicial processes like the Nürnberg trials.

The TRC was set up under the Promotion of National Unity and Reconciliation Act, No. 34 of 1995, and its hearings started in 1996. It aimed to bear witness to, record, and in some cases grant amnesty to the perpetrators of crimes relating to human rights violations, while also offering reparation and rehabilitation to the victims. The commission worked through three committees: The Human Rights Violations Committee, The Reparation and Rehabilitation Committee, and The Amnesty Committee.

The commission's findings and the subsequent report presented to President Mandela in October 1998 revealed that approximately 21,000 victims testified, and amnesty was granted in 849 cases out of 7,112 applications. The report highlighted the massive destruction of records between 1990 and 1994 and named individual perpetrators, proposing detailed recommendations for a reparations program, societal and political system reforms, and the preservation of the commission's work by archiving its documents.

Despite the initial support and the significant impact of the TRC in promoting forgiveness and reconciliation, criticisms and reservations emerged from all sides. Mandela noted these but accepted the report. In the years following Mandela's presidency, work on the TRC's recommendations largely ceased, and for many South Africans, the TRC came to represent a betrayal. The underpinning strategy of reconciliation began to unravel, leading to calls for revisiting the recommendations and completing the commission's unfinished business.

The TRC remains a significant part of South Africa's transition from apartheid to democracy, embodying the complexities and challenges of reconciling a deeply divided society. Its approach to restorative justice over retributive justice and its emphasis on uncovering the truth and facilitating forgiveness have been influential worldwide, even as debates continue about its effectiveness and the implementation of its recommendations.

The Boycott and Its Implications

The Simon Commission, officially named the Indian Statutory Commission, was established by the British government in 1927 to suggest constitutional reforms for British India. However, the commission faced immediate opposition from Indian national leaders and freedom activists due to its all-British composition, which was seen as an insult to Indians who argued their destiny could not be decided without their representation.

The decision to boycott the Simon Commission was a unifying moment for Indian political movements, including the Indian National Congress and the Muslim League led by M.A. Jinnah. The boycott was decided upon during the Indian National Congress session in Madras in 1927, demonstrating a pan-Indian rejection of British attempts to impose reforms without Indian consent. This collective stance underscored the demand for greater Indian participation in governance and the drafting of constitutional reforms.

The boycott had significant implications for marginalized voices in the national discourse. For instance, Dr. B.R. Ambedkar, representing the marginalized Dalit community, submitted a report on behalf of the Bahishkrit Hitakarini Sabha on the education of depressed classes in the Bombay Presidency, highlighting the need for their representation in any discussion on constitutional reforms. The widespread protests and the subsequent political mobilization emphasized the role of marginalized communities in the national struggle, drawing attention to their demands for equality and representation.

One of the most notable incidents associated with the commission's visit was the protest led by Lala Lajpat Rai in Lahore, where he was severely injured by the police and later died due to his injuries. This event sparked more opposition to British rule and showed India's fight for self-rule.

Ultimately, the Simon Commission's recommendations led to the Government of India Act 1935, which laid the groundwork for many parts of the Indian Constitution. The Act called for responsible government at the provincial level but maintained significant British control, reflecting a compromise rather than a full concession to Indian demands.

The Boycott's Impact

Highlighted Marginalized Demands: The boycott brought to the forefront the demands and needs of marginalized communities, such as Dalits, by highlighting their absence in the Commission's considerations and the broader political dialogue.

Increased Political Mobilization: Marginalized communities became more politically mobilized and active, using the boycott as a platform to voice their grievances and demand equal representation in the political process.

Dr. B.R. Ambedkar's Advocacy: Dr. Ambedkar's engagement with the Commission, such as submitting a report on behalf of the Bahishkrit Hitakarini Sabha, emphasized the need for specific reforms to address the issues faced by depressed classes, thus securing a place for marginalized voices in discussions on constitutional reforms.

Unified Opposition Against Discrimination: The boycott unified various segments of Indian society, including marginalized groups, against the common cause of British discrimination, fostering a sense of unity and shared purpose among diverse social groups.

Spotlight on Systemic Inequalities: The national and international attention garnered by the boycott illuminated the systemic inequalities and injustices faced by marginalized communities, forcing both British and Indian leaders to acknowledge and address these issues in future reforms.

The Precursor to Future Legislation: The widespread opposition and the specific demands raised by marginalized communities during the boycott period laid the groundwork for future legislation aimed at social reform and equal representation, influencing the content of the Government of India Act 1935 and later the Indian Constitution.

Empowerment Through Representation: The events surrounding the Simon Commission boycott empowered marginalized communities by demonstrating the impact of collective action and advocacy, setting a precedent for future movements aimed at achieving social justice and equality.

The boycott of the Simon Commission is a pivotal moment in the Indian freedom struggle and marked a significant step towards inclusive representation in the national discourse, particularly for marginalized communities seeking recognition and rights within the evolving political landscape of India.

Conclusion

The recommendations of the Simon Commission, despite the widespread boycott and criticism, inadvertently laid the groundwork for a systematic classification of Indian society into various categories, notably the Scheduled Castes (SC) and Scheduled Tribes (ST), and the Backward Classes (BC), listed in the Government of India Act of 1935. This classification recognized the deep-seated social stratifications and aimed to address the historical injustices and disparities faced by these communities.

The categorisation into SC, ST, and BC was a significant move towards acknowledging the varied layers of social exclusion and discrimination experienced by different groups within Indian society. It recognized the existence of "untouchables", "semi-touchables", and "fully touchables", with tribal communities often standing as exceptions due to their distinct social and cultural practices.

This basic classification system was pivotal in shaping the policies and affirmative actions in independent India, including reservations in education, employment, and politics, to uplift these marginalised communities. But now, these categories have changed. Different communities are seen in different ways across India, showing how in society there is complex and varied.

The conclusion drawn from the Simon Commission's aftermath is that while the commission itself was met with significant opposition, its legacy through the Government of India Act 1935 had a lasting impact on the country's approach to addressing social inequality. It set a precedent for recognizing the need for targeted measures to ensure equality and justice for all, particularly for those historically marginalized and discriminated against in the intricate social hierarchy of India.

CHAPTER 3

Democracy's Foundation - Elected to Bombay Presidency as MLA

In a democracy, the foundation of governance is representation. This principle ensures that the will and interests of the people are reflected in the decisions made by those in power. Representation in a democratic context primarily takes three forms: elected representatives, god-given representatives, and self-made representatives.

Elected representatives are the cornerstone of democratic systems. They are chosen by the citizens through a process of voting, typically held at regular intervals. This process is fundamental to democracy because it provides a mechanism for the people to select leaders who reflect their preferences and values. Elected representatives are accountable to their constituents, and their primary responsibility is to advocate for the interests and welfare of those they represent. This form of representation is based on the premise that all eligible citizens should have a say in who governs them, thereby legitimising the authority of elected officials through the consent of the governed.

God-given representatives, on the other hand, have their authority from a divine or religious mandate. In this form of representation, leaders claim their right to govern based on religious texts, traditions, or the supposed will of a deity. This approach to governance is common in theocracies, where religious leaders also serve as political leaders, and the laws of the land are often based on religious doctrines. The legitimacy of god-given representatives is rooted in the belief systems of their followers, rather than through a democratic electoral process.

Self-made representatives emerge from among the people, often without formal election or divine sanction. These individuals claim to represent certain groups based on personal achievements, charisma, or by championing specific causes. While they may not hold official political office, self-made representatives can influence public opinion and policy through advocacy, activism, or by leading social movements. Their authority stems from their ability to mobilize support for their ideas and initiatives, making them a unique form of representation in the democratic landscape.

When Dr. B.R. Ambedkar became a Member of the Legislative Assembly (MLA) for the Bombay Presidency, it was a huge deal for Indian democracy. Imagine, for the first time, people who had been ignored and pushed aside were going to have their voice heard where it really mattered—in making laws. Dr. Ambedkar stepping into this role was like opening a door for many who hadn't been invited to the conversation about their own country's future.

This was especially important because India was fighting for two big things at the same time: freedom from British rule and fairness for everyone, no matter their background. Dr. Ambedkar being elected wasn't just about him. It was about making politics more open to everyone, giving a chance to those who had been left out.

To really get what's going on here, it helps to think about what representation means. In a democracy, being able to vote for leaders is key. These leaders are supposed to stand up for us, and make sure our needs and wants are considered when decisions are made. But there are different ways people can end up in these powerful positions. Some believe their authority comes from a higher power, others might take charge because they see a need and they have the will and the support to do something about it. Then there are those, like Dr. Ambedkar, who get there because people vote for them, believing they're the right person to speak up for their community.

Dr. Ambedkar getting into the Bombay Legislative Assembly was a turning point. It showed that democracy in India was ready to grow, to include voices from corners of society that had been quiet for too long. His win was not just a personal victory but a signal that things were changing, that the fight for a fairer society was getting some real traction.

What makes elected leaders like Dr. Ambedkar so special in a democracy is pretty straightforward. They're chosen by us, "We the people". That means they have to listen to what we want and need, and they're supposed to make sure our voices are heard in government. This is a bit different from leaders who claim they're chosen by divine right or those who carve out a space for themselves based on their personality or achievements. Elected leaders have a job because we give it to them, and they answer to us.

In the big picture, what Dr. Ambedkar did for democracy in India goes way beyond just being elected. He used his position to push for changes that made society more fair, fighting for people who had been treated unfairly for way too long. His work laid down some important ground rules for what India could become: a place where everyone has a say, where being fair isn't just an idea but something we do.

The Scriptural Basis of Governance

In the Bible, specifically in the Book of Daniel, chapter 2, verse 4, there's a fascinating story about a dream that King Nebuchadnezzar of Babylon had. He sees a giant statue made of different materials: its head is of gold, its chest and arms of silver, its belly and thighs of bronze, its legs of iron, and its feet partly of iron and partly of baked clay. This statue is struck by a stone, not made by human hands, which causes the statue to break into pieces and get blown away by the wind without leaving a trace. Then, the stone that struck the statue becomes a huge mountain that fills the whole earth.

This dream, as explained by Daniel, represents successive kingdoms—each part of the statue stands for a different kingdom. Starting with the golden head, which symbolises Nebuchadnezzar's empire, Babylon, each material represents empires that will come after, each with its strengths and weaknesses. The gold represents the wealth and strength of Babylon, the silver its successors who might have less splendor, the bronze a further decline in nobility, and the iron and clay a mix of strength and fragility in the final kingdoms.

What's interesting about this metaphor is how it relates to the idea of governance and representation. Each kingdom, or material, has its unique qualities and vulnerabilities, just like different forms of government and leadership in our world. Some might be strong in one area but weak in another. This idea can be applied to how we think about governments and their leaders—no one system or leader is perfect; each has its pros and cons.

This story from Daniel 2:4 offers a way to think about the transition from divinely sanctioned rulers, like kings who believed they were chosen by God, to democratically elected representatives. Just as the statue's materials change and become mixed, governance has evolved from monarchies (where power is inherited and supposed to be blessed by divine right) to democracies (where leaders are chosen and blessed by the people).

The statue's destruction by a stone "not made by human hands" suggests a move towards something different—a new kind of kingdom or governance that is not established by the same old ways of power and domination. It hints at a form of governance that is more inclusive, representing a foundation built on principles that consider the well-being of all, not just the powerful.

In a broader sense, this scripture points to the idea that all human systems of governance have their time and place but are ultimately imperfect and temporary. It encourages us to think about how we can build societies that are just, equitable, and serve the needs of everyone, not just a select few. This is a useful reflection when considering the role of elected representatives in democracy, as it emphasizes the need for systems that truly represent and benefit all members of society.

Concept Of Governance And Representation

The story of the statue from Daniel 2:4, made of different materials and eventually destroyed, offers a unique way to think about how countries are run and how leaders are chosen. Long ago, many people believed that kings and queens were chosen by a higher power, and that's why they had the right to rule. This is what we mean by "divinely sanctioned rulers." Basically, it was thought that God picked these leaders, so people should follow them.

But over time, things started to change. Just like the statue in the dream was struck down and replaced by something new, the way countries decide on their leaders has also changed. Nowadays, in many places, leaders aren't seen as chosen by God but are elected by the people living in that country. This is what we call "democratically elected representatives." Instead of one person or family being in charge because they're believed to be chosen by a higher power, leaders are chosen through voting, where everyone gets to have a say.

This shift is kind of like moving from the gold part of the statue (representing strong, wealthy, but unchangeable kingdoms) to the stone that wasn't made by human hands. It's a big change from the idea that power comes from divine right to believing that power comes from the people themselves. It's a more inclusive way of deciding who gets to make important decisions for everyone, making sure that all different voices and opinions can be heard.

In a way, this story from Daniel can help us understand why it's so important to have leaders who represent what everyone wants and needs, not just what one person or a small group thinks is best. It reminds us that no one way of governing is perfect and that sometimes, new ways of doing things can be better for everyone.

Dr. B.R. Ambedkar's Electoral Victory

Dr. B.R. Ambedkar's journey to being elected to the Bombay Legislative Assembly is a story of determination, resilience, and a deep commitment to social justice. Born in 1891 into a Dalit family, Ambedkar faced the sting of caste-based discrimination from a very young age. But he didn't allow these obstacles to shape what was to come. They only made him more determined to stand up for the rights of the Dalit community, who faced discrimination in all parts of society.

Ambedkar's early life was marked by remarkable academic achievement despite the odds stacked against him. His quest for education took him from Bombay to the United States and then to the United Kingdom, where he earned multiple degrees, including a doctorate in law. This educational journey wasn't just about personal achievement. For Ambedkar, it was about acquiring the tools he needed to challenge and change the systemic injustices faced by Dalits in India.

Returning to India in the 1920s, Ambedkar found a country in the hero's of a struggle for independence from British rule. Yet, he saw that this fight for freedom often overlooked the plight of Dalits, who suffered under oppressive caste hierarchies that denied them basic human rights. Ambedkar's vision went beyond just political independence from the British. He envisioned a truly liberated India where Dalits enjoyed the same rights and opportunities as everyone else.

With this vision, Ambedkar came into public life and spoke up, using his legal knowledge and deep understanding of India's social systems to work for change. He championed education for Dalits as a means of empowerment, fought for their right to access public water sources and temples, and advocated for fair labor practices. However, Ambedkar knew that for real change to happen, he needed a platform where he could directly influence laws and policies.

In 1936, Ambedkar started a political party called the Independent Labour Party. This party fought for the rights of the "Depressed Classes," which are now known as Scheduled Castes and Scheduled Tribes. The next year, in 1937, his party did very well in the elections for the Bombay Legislative Assembly. They won many seats, showing that they had a lot of support from the people.

Ambedkar worked hard to make life better for people who were treated badly because of their caste. He fought to change unfair laws and to make new ones that would protect these people's rights. One of his big achievements was the Poona Pact of 1932. This agreement made sure that people from depressed classes would have their own representatives in the government.

Dr. Ambedkar's efforts were not just about winning elections. He played a big role in helping India become a free country and in writing its constitution. He worked to make sure that the Constitution protected everyone's rights, no matter their caste. He also held important positions in the government, where he continued to fight for equality.

Ambedkar's election was more than a personal win; it was a symbol of hope for millions of Dalits. It showed that change was possible and that the barriers of caste could be challenged through the democratic process. This victory set the stage for Ambedkar's future contributions to India, including his pivotal role in drafting the Indian Constitution and his tireless advocacy for Dalit rights.

The Societal Impact

Dr. B.R. Ambedkar's work had a big impact on society, especially for people who were treated unfairly because of their caste. He helped change how society thought about and treated these people. Before Ambedkar, people from lower castes were not allowed to do many things that others could. They couldn't drink water from the same places, go to the same schools, or even enter temples. Ambedkar fought against these rules and worked to get equal rights for everyone.

One of his biggest fights was for the right to education for everyone, no matter their caste. He believed that education was very important for making people's lives better. He also worked to improve women's rights and made sure that the Indian Constitution protected these rights.

However, Ambedkar faced many challenges as a leader who represented marginalized people. Many people did not agree with his ideas or his work. Sometimes, people from higher castes did not support his efforts to change unfair laws. Even in his own political career, there were challenges. For example, in India's first general elections in 1952, despite his popularity and the respect he had earned, he did not win a seat in the lower house of Parliament. This showed the difficulty of changing people's minds and the strong opposition he faced. But this did not stop him. He was later elected to the Rajya Sabha, which is the upper house of Parliament, where he continued his work until he passed away in 1956 (Constitution of India).

Despite these challenges, Ambedkar's work left a lasting impact. He showed that change is possible, even in the face of big challenges. Today, Ambedkar is remembered as a hero for his fight against inequality and his work to make India a better place for everyone. His birthday is a public holiday, United Nation had declared it as International Knowledge Day and people all over the country remember and honor his contributions to Indian society and the world.

The Concept of Elected Representatives

In a democratic society, elected representatives play a critical role. The people choose them through elections to act on their behalf in the government. These representatives can include members of Parliament, state legislatures, and local councils. Their primary role is to represent the interests and will of the people who elected them.

Responsibilities of Elected Representatives:

Lawmaking: One of the main responsibilities of elected representatives is to propose, debate, and vote on new laws or changes to existing laws. They must consider the needs and wishes of their constituents while also keeping in mind the greater good of the country or community.

Representation: Representatives are expected to be the voice of their constituents in the government. They bring the issues, concerns, and opinions of the people from their district or area to the attention of the larger government body. This could involve advocating for more resources for their area or opposing policies that could harm their constituents.

Oversight: Elected officials have the duty to oversee government programs and spending to ensure they are effective and that taxpayer money is being used responsibly. This includes reviewing the actions of the executive branch of the government and holding them accountable through hearings or investigations.

Constituent Services: Helping constituents navigate government services and bureaucracy is another key role. This might involve assisting with paperwork, addressing grievances related to government services, or providing information about government programs.

Policy Development: Representatives contribute to the development and shaping of policies that impact various sectors such as health, education, economy, and environment. They must research, understand complex issues, and develop policies that seek to improve the welfare of society.

Public Engagement: Engaging with the public is crucial. This can include holding town hall meetings, being active on social media, and attending local events. Through these interactions, representatives can understand the public's views and explain their positions and the work they are doing.

Elected representatives face the challenge of balancing their constituents' immediate needs with the entire population's long-term interests. They must also navigate the complexities of political alliances, party positions, and their convictions and values.

Comparison With God-Given And Self-Made Representatives

In comparing elected representatives with god-given or self-made representatives, three key aspects come into play: legitimacy, accountability, and public service.

- **Legitimacy**

  Elected representatives gain their legitimacy from the electoral process. This means that people choose them through voting, which is a fundamental part of democracy. Their authority to make decisions comes from the fact that a majority of the community has given them this right.

  God-given or hereditary representatives, such as monarchs in a traditional monarchy, derive their legitimacy from religious or cultural beliefs. The belief here is that their right to rule is granted by a higher power or passed down through family lines.

  Self-made representatives, like dictators or leaders who seize power through non-democratic means, claim legitimacy through their control over the state or government, often backed by military force. Their claim to authority is based on something other than public consent.

- **Accountability**

  Elected representatives are accountable to the people who elect them. They must listen to their constituents' concerns and can be voted out of office in the next election if the people are not satisfied with their performance. This creates a system where representatives are motivated to serve the public interest.

  God-given or hereditary leaders are traditionally seen as accountable to a higher power or bound by duty to their lineage rather than directly to the people. In many cases, there are limited mechanisms for public accountability, although modern constitutional monarchies often blend hereditary leadership with democratic institutions to ensure some level of public accountability.

Self-made representatives, on the other hand, may not have any formal accountability to the public. Their power often rests on force, and public dissent may be suppressed. Accountability may come from within the governing elite rather than the general public.

- **Public Service**

Elected representatives, because of their need for re-election and accountability to the electorate, are often motivated to engage in public service and to implement policies that benefit the public. Their office success is closely tied to their ability to meet the needs and expectations of their constituents.

God-given or hereditary leaders may engage in public service as part of their duty or role. Their approach to governance and public service can vary widely, depending on personal values, traditions, and the influence of advisory bodies or democratic institutions.

Self-made leaders might undertake public service initiatives to gain legitimacy and support among the population or to consolidate their power. However, their approach to public service can be heavily influenced by their interests, the need to maintain control, and the dynamics within their supporting elite.

The Importance of Democratic Representation

The importance of democratic representation has grown over time with an increasing emphasis on inclusivity and equality. In a democracy, the idea is that everyone should have a voice in how they are governed. This means that all groups in society, regardless of their background, income, gender, or beliefs, should have the chance to be represented and have a say in the political process.

- **Inclusivity**

  Inclusivity in democratic representation means making sure that all parts of society can participate fully in the political process. This includes efforts to remove barriers that might prevent people from voting or running for office. For example, providing voting materials in different languages can help people who speak those languages feel more included in the election process. Making public buildings accessible to people with disabilities is another way to ensure everyone can participate.

- **Equality**

  Equality means that everyone's vote has the same weight and that everyone has an equal chance to be heard. In practice, achieving this can be challenging. For instance, people with more money can sometimes have a louder voice in politics, through donations to campaigns or by funding their campaigns. To address this, many democracies have laws limiting how much money can be given to political campaigns and require reporting on where the money comes from.

- **Evolution of Ideas**

  Over time, the ideals of inclusivity and equality have led to changes in laws and practices to make politics more accessible to everyone. For example, the right to vote has been extended to more groups over time, including women and minority groups, in many countries. There have also been efforts to make elected bodies more reflective of society's diversity, such as measures to increase the representation of women and minorities in parliament.

These changes are based on the belief that a government is more fair and effective when it represents the whole of society, not just a few parts. When everyone has a say, the government can make better decisions that benefit everyone. This focus on inclusivity and equality helps to strengthen democracy and make it more resilient.

Bridging The Gap

Bridging the gap between the government and the people, especially for marginalized communities, is crucial for creating a fair and just society. This means making sure that all people, no matter their background or situation, can communicate with the government and have their needs and concerns addressed.

Understanding the Gap

The gap often exists because people in marginalized communities may not have the same access to political processes as others. This can be due to many reasons, such as poverty, lack of education, or historical discrimination. They might also feel, work and act in a way that the government does not represent or understand their interests.

Ways to Bridge the Gap

Community Representation: Ensuring that these communities have representatives in government can help bridge the gap. When people see themselves reflected in their leaders, they are more likely to feel connected and listened to. These representatives can advocate for policies and programs that address the specific needs of their communities.

Accessible Government: The government needs to be accessible to everyone. This means providing information in various languages, making public buildings accessible to people with disabilities, and offering various ways for people to contact their representatives.

Public Engagement: Governments can hold public meetings, forums, and consultations in different communities, especially in areas that are often overlooked. This allows community members to express their concerns directly to those in power.

Education and Outreach: Educating people about their rights and how the government works can empower them to participate in the political process. Government agencies and non-government organizations can offer programs that help people learn how to advocate for themselves and their communities.

Feedback Mechanisms: Creating mechanisms for feedback, such as surveys or public comment periods, can help the government understand what issues are most important to people. This feedback must be considered and used to make decisions.

Support for Advocacy Groups: Advocacy groups play a key role in representing and fighting for the rights of marginalized communities. The government can support these groups by providing funding, information, and access to decision-makers.

Bridging this gap is important for democracy to function properly. When everyone has a voice, and their concerns are addressed, it leads to better policies that reflect the diverse needs of the entire population. It also builds trust between the government and the people, making it more likely that people will support and follow government policies.

Ambedkar's Vision for an Inclusive Democracy

Dr. Ambedkar's vision for an inclusive democracy in India was groundbreaking. He believed that democracy should work for everyone, not just for certain groups. His work, especially in drafting the Indian Constitution, laid the foundation for a society based on equality, justice, and freedom.

- **Drafting the Constitution**

  As the chairman of the Drafting Committee for the Indian Constitution, Dr. Ambedkar played a pivotal role in shaping the future of India's democracy. He ensured that the Constitution guaranteed rights for all citizens, regardless of their caste, religion, or gender. This was a significant step forward in creating an inclusive society where everyone has the opportunity to participate fully.

- **Advocating for Social Justice**

  Dr. Ambedkar's fight for social justice is well-documented. He tirelessly worked to end the caste system and improve the lives of the marginalized, particularly those in the Dalit community, who had been excluded and discriminated against for centuries. He advocated for equal rights, access to education, and the right to public spaces for everyone.

- **Equality and Protection Under Law**

  One of Dr. Ambedkar's major contributions was his insistence on equality and protection under the law for all citizens. The Constitution includes provisions to protect against discrimination and to uplift marginalized communities through affirmative action. These measures were radical at the time and showcased his commitment to building a fair and just society.

- **Women's Rights**

  Dr. Ambedkar was also a strong advocate for women's rights. He fought for the Hindu Code Bill, which aimed to improve the rights of women regarding marriage, inheritance, and property. Though he faced significant opposition, his efforts laid the groundwork for future reforms that would grant more rights to women.

- **Legacy**

  Dr. Ambedkar's legacy continues to influence India today. His vision for an inclusive democracy where everyone has equal rights and opportunities remains a guiding principle for the nation. His work on the Constitution ensures that India strives towards a more equitable society, and his advocacy for social justice inspires new generations to continue the fight for equality.

Legislative Work And Advocacy

Dr. Ambedkar's legislative work and advocacy significantly reshaped the concept of representation in India, making the political system more accessible and fair for previously marginalized groups.

- **Expanding Representation**

  Dr. Ambedkar worked towards expanding the idea of representation to include all segments of society, not just the privileged or majority groups. He played a key role in ensuring that the Indian Constitution provided reserved seats in Parliament and state legislatures for Scheduled Castes and Scheduled Tribes. This move ensured that these communities could elect their own representatives, who would understand and advocate for their interests.

- **Advocacy for Equal Voting Rights**

  He was a strong advocate for universal adult suffrage, which granted voting rights to all adults, regardless of caste, class, or gender. This was a radical idea at the time, given the deep social hierarchies that existed. His insistence on equal voting rights was crucial in making democracy in India more inclusive. Universal voting rights are implemented for before the so-called Western developed societies adopted this idea.

- **Empowering Marginalized Communities**

  Dr. Ambedkar's advocacy went beyond the halls of legislation. He worked on the ground to educate and empower marginalized communities about their rights and the importance of political participation. By raising awareness and encouraging active participation, he helped ensure that representation in India wasn't just a matter of filling seats but involved the active and meaningful participation of all sections of society.

- **Legislative Reforms**

  Through various legislative reforms, Dr. Ambedkar sought to dismantle the barriers that prevented marginalized communities from accessing their rights and participating fully in society. His work on labor laws, for example, helped improve the working conditions and rights of workers, many of whom belonged to disadvantaged communities.

- **Impact on Political Culture**

  The impact of Dr. Ambedkar's work on representation in India is profound. By advocating for policies and laws that ensured more inclusive representation, he helped change the political culture of the nation. Representation in India's democracy now includes a wide array of voices from different social, economic, and cultural backgrounds, moving closer to Dr. Ambedkar's vision of equality and justice for all.

Representation of the People Act

The "Representation of the People Act" plays a key role in safeguarding the integrity of India's democratic system by setting strict eligibility criteria for elected officials. This law is crucial in preventing conflicts of interest and ensuring that representatives are fully committed to their public duties without any undue influence from other paid positions or benefits.

One notable application of this law was in 2006, involving Sonia Gandhi. She resigned from her position in the Lok Sabha after it was found that she held an office of profit, which the Act identifies as a potential conflict of interest that could interfere with her duties as an elected official. Her resignation highlighted the law's effectiveness in enforcing ethical standards among politicians.

This Act underscores the commitment to transparency and accountability in Indian politics. It reflects the foundational principles of democracy that Dr. Ambedkar emphasized—equality before the law and the necessity of a clean and accountable governance system. By strictly regulating the qualifications and conduct of public servants, the Act helps ensure that all representatives remain dedicated to the welfare of their constituents, free from any personal or financial entanglements that could hinder their decision-making.

This incident not only demonstrates the enforcement of the law but also serves as a reminder of the ongoing vigilance required to maintain the democratic values embedded in India's political system. The "Representation of the People Act" thus remains a critical tool in upholding the democratic structure that seeks to serve all citizens equitable.

Conclusion

India did something really big in 1950. Right after becoming free from British rule, it said every adult could vote. This means if you were grown up, no matter if you were a man or woman, rich or poor, or what your job was, you could vote. This was a huge deal because even before many countries in the West did this, India made sure everyone had a voice in choosing who ran the country.

With so many different kinds of people living in the country, from so many different places and backgrounds, everyone has the right to say, *"I want this person to be in charge."* That was pretty bold and showed everyone that India cared about what fairness means.

So, in a way, India showed the world how to be fair by letting everyone have a say through voting. It wasn't just about making laws; it was about making sure everyone felt they belonged and had a part in shaping the future. *That's something to be really proud of, isn't it?*

CHAPTER 4

The First Nonviolent Movement - Mahad Water Drinking Movement

Water: The Essential Element of Life

Water is fundamental to all life. Every plant, animal, and human on this planet relies on it for survival. It's not just a resource; it's the very basis of life. The human body, for instance, is made up of about 60% to 70%of its weight as water, which it needs for various functions such as digestion, temperature regulation, and transport of nutrients.

Beyond its biological importance, water is crucial for daily life activities. From cooking and cleaning to agriculture and industry, water supports virtually every aspect of human civilisation. It's a critical factor in economic development, health, and sustainability.

However, access to clean and safe water remains a significant challenge for many around the world. This issue of access is not just about physical availability but also about social equity. The right to water is recognised by the United Nations as a human right, vital to the realisation of all other human rights. It underscores the importance of managing this critical resource in a way that is sustainable and equitable, ensuring that everyone, regardless of their background or economic status, has access to safe water necessary for a healthy life.

In contexts like Mahad in 1927, where certain communities were denied access to clean water based on their caste, the struggle for water access highlights a profound fight for equality and justice. It shows how essential water is, not just for survival, but as a right that should be equally available to all individuals, serving as a foundation for social equity and human dignity.

The caste system in India is a form of social stratification where individuals are born into a specific social group that determines their occupation, status, and potential relationships. This system has been a part of Indian society for thousands of years and is deeply rooted in cultural, religious, and historical practices. Here's a simplified explanation of the caste system and the discrimination that arose from it, particularly during the 1920s when India was under British rule.

During the 1920s, India's societal structure was deeply influenced by the caste system, which segregated communities into hierarchical groups based on birth. This period was marked by significant caste-based discrimination, particularly against the Dalits, who were considered the lowest in the caste hierarchy and faced severe social and economic exclusion.

People were discriminated against based on their caste for several reasons:

- **Religious beliefs:** The caste system was traditionally linked to religious practices, which suggested that one's birth in a certain caste was a result of their past actions (karma) and determined their place in society.
- **Social control:** By keeping groups separated and hierarchical, the upper castes could maintain control over resources and power, ensuring that the lower castes remained subservient.
- **Economic benefits:** Upper castes had access to better jobs, more land, and educational opportunities, which they wanted to preserve for their own group.

The caste system enforced a rigid social order where Dalits were denied access to essential public resources, including water, temples, and educational institutions. This denial was not just a social practice but was often reinforced by law and policy, which codified the marginalization of lower castes and supported the privileges of the upper castes.

Background of the Mahad Satyagraha

In the town of Mahad, Maharashtra, there was a public water tank known as the Chavdar tank. At the time, Dalits, who were placed at the lowest level of the caste hierarchy, were strictly forbidden from using this tank. The upper castes, who dominated society, labeled Dalits as 'untouchable' and believed any contact with them would contaminate their purity. This belief extended to the use of public amenities, including water tanks, which were essential for daily life.

The exclusion of Dalits from the Chavdar tank was not just a local practice but a visible sign of the widespread discrimination they faced throughout India. Such practices were enforced both socially and occasionally through local laws, reflecting deep-seated prejudices that had been entrenched for centuries.

Dr. B.R. Ambedkar, a prominent person from Dalit community educated in the United States and the United Kingdom, recognized the need to challenge these injustices directly. He was uniquely positioned as a lawyer and a scholar to understand the intersection of law, rights, and social practices. Ambedkar believed that for Dalits to gain respect and equal status in Indian society, they needed to challenge the most visible symbols of discrimination.

Ambedkar's choice of nonviolent protest was inspired by the effectiveness of similar movements globally that advocated for civil rights and social change without resorting to violence. His strategy was influenced by the growing discourse around civil rights, which advocated for achieving social goals through peaceful means. By choosing nonviolence, Ambedkar aimed to highlight the unjust nature of caste discrimination while maintaining moral high ground, aiming to garner wider support from different sections of society, including sympathetic members of upper castes and the colonial British authorities who might be swayed by peaceful methods rather than violent rebellion.

The timing of the Mahad Satyagraha was also critical. India in the 1920s was a period of intense social and political activity, with various groups mobilizing to demand greater rights and freedoms from the British colonial rule. In this environment, Ambedkar saw an opportunity to push the boundaries of what was socially acceptable and to force the public and the authorities to confront the inhumanity of untouchability.

Mahad Satyagraha: A Landmark in Nonviolent Struggle

The Mahad Satyagraha, led by Dr. B.R. Ambedkar on March 20, 1927, was a significant event that highlighted the struggle for Dalit rights in India. Dr. Ambedkar, a prominent Dalit leader and social reformer, organized this movement to assert the rights of Dalits to access public water in Mahad, Maharashtra. This event was not just about drinking water from a public tank but was a symbolic act against the widespread discrimination and injustice faced by Dalits.

Mahad, a town in Maharashtra, was chosen for this protest due to its prominent public water tank, the Chavdar tank, which was traditionally off-limits to Dalits. Despite laws that suggested equality, local social practices enforced by upper-caste Hindus barred Dalits from using this tank. The denial was a clear symbol of the widespread discrimination based on caste, perceived impurity, and social exclusion.

The event was carefully planned. Dr. Ambedkar and his team published an announcement inviting Dalits to gather at Mahad for a conference. On the day of the Satyagraha, Dr. Ambedkar addressed a large gathering of Dalits, explaining the importance of fighting for their rights and the need for direct action to challenge social norms. Following his speech, he led the crowd to the tank. In a defining moment, Dr. Ambedkar touched the water of the Chavdar tank, and then he and thousands of his followers drank from it. This act was revolutionary because it directly confronted the oppressive social norms of the time.

The reaction from the upper-caste community was immediate and severe. They perceived the Dalits' use of the tank as a pollution of their water source. In retaliation, they performed purification rituals and even resorted to violence against the Dalits. The opposition was not just social but also legal. The upper castes filed a lawsuit to prevent Dalits from accessing the tank, arguing that it was private property. This legal battle continued until 1937, when the Bombay High Court finally ruled in favor of the Dalits' right to use the tank.

Dr. Ambedkar's leadership in the Mahad Satyagraha was crucial. He not only challenged physical barriers but also fought against the psychological chains that had bound the Dalit community for centuries. By asserting their right to drink water from the public tank, Dr. Ambedkar was asserting the Dalits' right to equality and dignity.

The Mahad Satyagraha was more than just a protest for water rights; it was a critical step towards social reform. It highlighted the need for systemic change in Indian society and sparked numerous other movements and legal challenges against caste discrimination. The courage shown by the Dalits at Mahad had a lasting impact, inspiring future generations to continue the fight for equality and justice.

The Catalyst for Change: Municipal Resolutions and Social Injustice

In Mahad, Maharashtra, the Chavdar tank represented more than just a water source; it was a symbol of deeply entrenched social injustice. This public tank, accessible to animals and people of higher castes, starkly illustrated the discrimination faced by the untouchables, or Dalits, who were systematically denied access due to prevailing caste prejudices.

The prohibition against Dalits using the Chavdar tank was not just a matter of tradition but was enforced by the upper caste members of the community with little to no official intervention against such practices. The denial of access to something as basic as water underlined the extreme marginalisation of Dalits and highlighted the failures of societal and governmental systems to protect fundamental human rights.

Municipal Resolutions

The situation began to change with the intervention of legislative and municipal bodies, which started to recognize the severity of caste-based exclusions. On August 4, 1923, the Bombay Legislative Council, prompted by social reformers and activists, passed a resolution advocating for the rights of untouchables to access public watering places, schools, and other amenities. This resolution aimed to enforce the notion that public amenities funded by the government should be accessible to all, irrespective of caste.

Following the council's resolution, the Mahad Municipality passed its own resolution in January 1924, which specifically declared that the Chavdar tank was to be accessible to all citizens, including the Dalits. However, despite these official mandates, the actual implementation faced significant resistance. The upper castes in Mahad, who had long viewed the tank as a symbol of their social privilege, opposed these changes vehemently.

Resistance and Social Dynamics

The resistance from the upper castes was rooted in deeply held beliefs about purity and pollution—a core aspect of the caste system where physical or even symbolic contact with Dalits was considered polluting. This belief system was so ingrained that the mere presence of Dalits at the tank was seen as contaminating the water, thereby rendering it impure for the use by higher castes.

This social and cultural backdrop set the stage for what would become a significant confrontation. The municipal resolutions were a critical first step, but without enforcement and acceptance by the local community, they did little to alleviate the plight of the Dalits. The lack of immediate change following these resolutions highlighted the gap between legislative action and social reality, underscoring the need for a more direct form of action and advocacy.

Dr. Ambedkar's Intervention

Recognizing that legislative changes were not sufficient to combat the deeply rooted social norms, Dr. B.R. Ambedkar saw an urgent need for direct action. He understood that challenging these norms would require more than just words; it needed a visible, impactful demonstration that would force society to confront its prejudices. This understanding led to the organization of the Mahad Satyagraha, which was not only about asserting the right to access water but also about challenging the very foundations of caste discrimination in a public and confrontational way.

The Mahad Satyagraha, therefore, was as much a response to the failures of the municipal resolutions as it was a statement against the broader social injustices inflicted upon the Dalits. By leading the movement to drink water from the Chavdar tank, Dr. Ambedkar was catalysing a change that would later ripple across India, influencing numerous other movements and leading to significant social reform.

Legislative Actions and Community Resistance

In the early 1920s, the plight of the Dalits, particularly their exclusion from basic public amenities, began to gain attention at both local and legislative levels. The Bombay Legislative Council, influenced by the growing discourse on civil rights and the efforts of reformers, took a significant step forward in 1923.

The Bombay Legislative Council's 1923 Resolution

On August 4, 1923, the Bombay Legislative Council passed a groundbreaking resolution. This resolution recommended that all public watering places, schools, and other public amenities should be accessible to the "untouchable" classes. This legislative move was aimed at dismantling the barriers imposed by traditional caste hierarchies that had long dictated access to basic needs.

Mahad Municipality's 1924 Resolution

Following the Bombay Presidency Council's resolution, the Mahad Municipality adopted its own resolution in January 1924, explicitly declaring the Chavdar tank in Mahad open to all citizens, irrespective of caste. This was a direct attempt to implement the legislative recommendation at a local level and to set a precedent that could lead to broader social reform.

Resistance from Caste Hindus

Despite these resolutions, their implementation met with stiff resistance from the upper-caste Hindus. The resistance was not merely a reluctance but a concerted effort to maintain the status quo that privileged them. The upper castes, who had historically controlled access to the tank, saw this move as a threat to their traditional authority and purity codes defined by the caste system.

The opposition was rooted in deeply entrenched beliefs about purity, pollution, and social hierarchy. The caste Hindus argued that allowing Dalits access to the tank would pollute the water, thus making it impure for their use. This belief system was so pervasive that it overrode the legal mandates aimed at ensuring equality and access for all.

The Gap Between Legislation and Social Practice

The gap between legislative intent and actual practice highlighted a significant challenge in transforming deeply ingrained social attitudes. Laws could mandate equality, but changing the hearts and minds of people who had lived by the caste system for generations proved much more difficult.

The failure to implement these resolutions reflected the limitations of legislation in effecting social change when not supported by community acceptance and active enforcement. It underscored the need for more direct action and visible advocacy to confront and change longstanding social norms.

The legislative resolutions of 1923 and 1924 were crucial in setting the legal framework for equality, but the strong resistance from caste Hindus demonstrated the complex interplay between law and social practice. This resistance ultimately set the stage for Dr. Ambedkar's Mahad Satyagraha, which aimed to not only assert Dalit rights to public spaces but also to challenge and change the societal attitudes that supported such discrimination. The Mahad Satyagraha would become a definitive moment in the fight against caste oppression, illustrating the power and necessity of direct action in the face of deep-seated social resistance.

Mobilizing the Dalits for the Mahad Satyagraha

The mobilization of Dalits for the Mahad Satyagraha was a meticulous and strategic process orchestrated by Dr. B.R. Ambedkar to challenge deeply rooted caste barriers in society. The aim was clear: to show that Dalits were entitled to the same rights as other citizens, including access to public utilities like water.

Spreading Awareness

The first step in the mobilization process was spreading awareness among the Dalit communities about the importance of the protest and what it symbolized. This was done primarily through word of mouth, a powerful tool in communities where interpersonal relationships were key to communication. Leaders and volunteers went from village to village, speaking at community gatherings and individual homes to educate Dalits about their rights and the significance of asserting these rights.

Dr. Ambedkar and his team also utilized pamphlets and other written materials to spread their message. These pamphlets were distributed widely and included information about the time and place of the protest, the objectives of the Satyagraha, and the broader implications of their fight for rights. The pamphlets served not only to inform but also to rally support, as they reached people who might not have been accessible through personal contact alone.

To ensure that the protest was effective and organized, numerous preparatory meetings were held. These meetings were crucial for logistical planning and for building a collective spirit among the participants. They provided spaces for potential protestors to come together, discuss their fears and hopes, and receive encouragement and instructions from leaders. These gatherings were instrumental in fostering a sense of unity and purpose among the Dalits, which was essential for the success of the Satyagraha.

Local leaders of the Dalit communities played a pivotal role in the mobilization effort. These leaders, who were deeply respected within their communities, acted as the primary points of contact between Dr. Ambedkar and the masses. Their endorsement of the Satyagraha lent credibility to the movement and was vital in persuading ordinary members of the community to participate. They were responsible for organizing groups, ensuring that people knew where and when to gather, and providing moral support to those who were hesitant.

Volunteers, including members of other castes who believed in the cause, were crucial to the mobilization efforts. They helped distribute materials, organize meetings, and spread the word beyond the Dalit communities. Their involvement was a testament to the growing recognition among the broader population that caste discrimination was a social evil that needed to be eradicated.

The ultimate objective of this extensive mobilization was not just to enable Dalits to drink water from the Chavdar tank but to challenge and change the public perception and treatment of Dalits in India. It aimed to demonstrate the strength and resolve of the Dalit community, and to assert their rights as equal citizens of India.

The Role of Dr. Ambedkar in the Mahad Satyagraha

Dr. B.R. Ambedkar's leadership in the Mahad Satyagraha was pivotal, transcending typical organizational roles to embody the spirit and direction of the movement. His involvement brought intellectual depth, strategic planning, and an impassioned moral perspective that profoundly influenced the Dalit community.

Dr. Ambedkar was not just a leader; he was a visionary who saw the Mahad Satyagraha as a critical step in the long battle against caste oppression. His deep understanding of the social, legal, and political frameworks of India allowed him to craft a movement that was both symbolic and substantive. Ambedkar's approach was to use the Satyagraha not only to address the specific issue of access to water but also to challenge the very foundations of caste discrimination.

One of Dr. Ambedkar's most significant contributions was his role as an educator and motivator. Through his speeches and writings, he provided the Dalit community with a clearer understanding of their rights and the injustices they faced. He educated them about the principles of equality and justice enshrined in various legal and philosophical texts, emphasizing that the denial of access to water was a violation of their basic rights.

Ambedkar's speeches were powerful and articulate, resonating deeply with his audience. He used these opportunities not just to inform but to empower, encouraging a sense of self-worth and dignity among the Dalits. His ability to connect complex legal and social theories with the everyday experiences of oppression made his messages both accessible and motivational.

Dr. Ambedkar was perceptive in positioning the Satyagraha within the broader context of global struggles for rights and equality. By framing the demand for water as part of a universal fight for dignity and human rights, he elevated the protest from a local issue to a symbol of the fight against oppression everywhere. This strategic framing helped to garner support from other communities and sympathetic observers both within and outside India.

Under Ambedkar's leadership, the Mahad Satyagraha became a unifying event for the Dalit community. He fostered a sense of solidarity that transcended local divisions and encouraged a collective identity among the Dalits. This unity was crucial in maintaining the nonviolent discipline of the Satyagraha, despite provocations and severe opposition from caste Hindus.

The effects of Dr. Ambedkar's leadership in the Mahad Satyagraha extended well beyond the immediate outcomes of the protest. His methods and messages influenced subsequent generations of Dalit leaders and activists, setting a precedent for future actions against caste-based injustices. The Satyagraha also had a significant impact on public discourse, pushing the issues of caste and discrimination into the national and international spotlight.

Violence and Court Intervention

Following the Mahad Satyagraha, where Dalits asserted their right to access the Chavdar tank, the response from the caste Hindus was severe and underscored the deep-seated prejudices that the protest sought to challenge. The backlash was not just verbal; it took a violently symbolic form that was aimed at both intimidating the Dalit community and reasserting caste boundaries.

After Dr. Ambedkar and his followers used the tank, some members of the upper caste community took drastic measures to "purify" the water, which they believed had been polluted by the Dalits. In a vivid display of caste beliefs in purity and pollution, they poured cow urine and dung into the tank. This act of desecration was intended to cleanse the tank of what they considered Dalit contamination. It was a stark reminder of the extreme lengths to which the caste Hindus were willing to go to maintain caste barriers.

The act of purifying the tank with cow urine and dung was deeply humiliating for the Dalit community. It not only reflected the literal and symbolic exclusion they faced but also the societal sanction of such exclusion. However, instead of deterring the Dalit movement, this reaction only strengthened their resolve. It highlighted the necessity of their struggle for equality and dignity in the face of such blatant disrespect.

The violent backlash and the desecration of the tank led to significant legal confrontations. The upper-caste community, in an effort to legally reinforce their stance, filed a lawsuit claiming that the tank was private property and that the Dalits had no right to use it. This legal battle extended the conflict from the streets into the courtroom.

The initial hearings were tense, and the court temporarily barred Dalits from accessing the tank, pending a final decision. However, this injunction was not the end of the legal struggle but the beginning of a protracted fight for justice in the courts.

After years of legal proceedings, the Bombay High Court delivered a landmark verdict in 1937. The court ruled in favor of the Dalits, establishing that the tank was a public resource and affirming the rights of Dalits to use it. This decision was a significant victory for the Dalit movement, as it not only granted them access to the water but also set a legal precedent for anti-discrimination laws concerning public amenities.

The fights over the Chavdar tank showed how the Dalits faced unfairness. They used peaceful protests to fight back. The events in Mahad made a big difference, leading to changes in laws and society in India.

The lawsuit was initiated by upper-caste leaders who sought to maintain exclusive access to the Chavdar tank by arguing that it was private property. Dr. Ambedkar and his team challenged this claim in court, arguing that the tank was a public resource and should be accessible to everyone, regardless of caste. This legal battle was not just about access to water but was symbolic of the broader fight against the social practices that underpinned untouchability in India.

The court proceedings were intense and complex, involving numerous legal arguments about rights, property, and public access. Ambedkar's legal strategy was to demonstrate that the exclusion of Dalits from the tank was not only morally indefensible but also legally unsustainable. He leveraged his extensive legal expertise to challenge the caste-based barriers enshrined in traditional practices, arguing for a reinterpretation of the laws in light of the principles of equality and justice.

The ruling by the Bombay High Court was groundbreaking. The court recognized the tank as a public utility, affirming that it was maintained by public funds and was intended for the use of the entire community, including Dalits. This decision was a clear legal acknowledgment that the exclusion of Dalits from public spaces was incompatible with the fundamental rights promised under the law.

The 1937 ruling had a profound impact beyond the immediate access to the Chavdar tank. It served as a precedent for other legal challenges against practices of untouchability and discrimination. The decision was a significant affirmation of the rights of Dalits to public spaces and resources, challenging longstanding social norms and contributing to the momentum for further legal and social reforms in India.

The Bombay High Court's decision also underscored the role of the judiciary in upholding civil rights and addressing social injustices. It highlighted the court's ability to act as a counterbalance to societal prejudices and to enforce constitutional principles of equality and justice.

This ruling continues to inspire those fighting for equality and justice, showing that change is possible when people come together to challenge injustice in a united way.

An incident resembling it,

The Miraculous Parting of the Red Sea: A Detailed Examination

The parting of the Red Sea is one of the most dramatic and significant events recounted in the Bible, specifically in the Book of Exodus. This story not only highlights a pivotal moment in the history of the Israelites but also serves as a profound example of faith, divine intervention, and the transition from slavery to freedom.

The Israelites, under the leadership of Moses, had been enslaved in Egypt for hundreds of years. Following God's command, Moses confronted the Pharaoh to release his people, which led to a series of divine interventions known as the Plagues of Egypt. Despite the severe plagues that devastated Egypt, Pharaoh's heart remained hardened until the final, most devastating plague — the death of the firstborns of Egypt — compelled him to release the Israelites.

However, soon after allowing Moses and his people to leave, Pharaoh's resolve wavered, and he pursued the Israelites with his army, intent on bringing them back into bondage. As the narrative unfolds, the Israelites find themselves facing the seemingly insurmountable obstacle of the Red Sea, with Pharaoh's army rapidly approaching from behind.

Faced with imminent danger and the Israelites' growing despair, Moses called upon God, who instructed him to raise his staff over the waters. Following this divine command, Moses stretched out his hand over the sea, and God drove the sea back with a strong east wind, turning it into dry land with waters forming walls on either side. This miraculous event allowed the Israelites to escape across the sea floor.

The parting of the Red Sea is symbolic of God's deliverance from oppression, showcasing His power over nature and His willingness to save His people from their enemies.

As the Egyptian army followed the Israelites into the seabed, their fate was sealed by another act of divine intervention. At Moses' command, the waters returned to their normal course, engulfing the Egyptian soldiers and their chariots, ensuring the Israelites' safe escape. This part of the story not only marks the deliverance of the Israelites from Egyptian pursuit but also serves as a powerful demonstration of divine justice and the ultimate futility of opposing God's will.

Theologically, the parting of the Red Sea has been interpreted as a baptismal symbol in Christian theology, representing the believers' passage from sin to salvation, mirroring the Israelites' transition from slavery to freedom. In Jewish tradition, it is celebrated during the Passover as a key act of God's salvation, a theme that is central to the holiday's observance.

Moses' role as a leader who acted with unyielding faith in God's promises is crucial. His actions and unwavering belief in God's assistance provide a template for biblical leadership and faith. The story also imparts lessons on the importance of obedience and trust in divine power, especially in seemingly impossible situations.

The story of the Red Sea parting has left a lasting impact on various cultures and religions. It has inspired numerous artistic representations, literary works, and films, each interpreting the event in unique ways that resonate with different audiences. The narrative continues to inspire faith communities around the world as a story of hope, liberation, and divine presence in human affairs. Works with water from historical importance.

Similarly, Jordan River,

The splitting of the Jordan River by Joshua, as described in the Bible, is another profound instance where a body of water is miraculously parted to allow God's people to pass through. This event occurs in the Book of Joshua, chapters 3 and 4, and serves as a significant theological and symbolic moment, marking the entry of the Israelites into the Promised Land.

After the death of Moses, Joshua became the leader of the Israelites and was tasked with leading them into the Promised Land, a land that God had promised to their ancestors. The journey to the Promised Land was not just a physical relocation but a fulfilment of a divine promise, representing a new phase in the life of the Israelites as a nation. However, the path to their new home was blocked by the Jordan River, which was at flood stage during harvest time, making it even more difficult to cross.

The Miracle at the Jordan

As instructed by God, Joshua told the priests to carry the Ark of the Covenant into the river ahead of the people. The Ark, which held the Tablets of the Law given to Moses, was a symbol of God's presence and covenant with the Israelites. As soon as the priests who carried the Ark touched the water's edge, the waters from upstream stopped flowing. It piled up in a heap a great distance away, at a town called Adam in the vicinity of Zarethan, while the water flowing down to the Sea of the Arabah (the Dead Sea) was completely cut off. This allowed the entire nation to cross over on dry ground.

The parting of the Jordan River mirrored the parting of the Red Sea, linking Joshua's leadership back to that of Moses and reinforcing the continuity of God's ongoing relationship with Israel. It acted as a sign that God's favor was with Joshua as it had been with Moses, and it reassured the people that they were still the chosen recipients of God's promises.

The stopping of Jordan's flow also served as a public demonstration of Joshua's divine authority and leadership, ensuring that the people would follow his command as they took possession of their new homeland. Moreover, the event highlighted themes of renewal and deliverance. Just as the crossing of the Red Sea symbolized the Israelites' release from Egyptian bondage, the crossing of the Jordan represented a transition from a nomadic existence to settling down in a land of their own.

To commemorate this miraculous event, Joshua commanded the Israelites to take twelve stones from Jordan's dry riverbed, one for each of the twelve tribes of Israel and set them up as a memorial at their encampment in Gilgal. These stones were to serve as a sign and a call to remembrance for all generations of the power of God and the importance of obedience to His will.

This moment is pivotal in the narrative of the Israelite's journey and its theological import, reinforcing themes of faith, divine intervention, and the fulfillment of promises. It stands as a testament to the transition into a phase of life that would define the character and destiny of the Israelite nation. Another works with water as a element of life.

Jesus of Nazareth in the Jordan River

According to the Gospels, Jesus came to the Jordan River to be baptised by John the Baptist. John was known for preaching about the coming of the Kingdom of God and was baptising people as a symbol of repentance and purification for the forgiveness of sins. Despite John's initial reluctance to baptize Jesus, saying that he felt unworthy and that it was Jesus who should baptize him, Jesus insisted. The act was to "fulfill all righteousness," indicating that it was part of God's divine plan and an example of obedience to God.

When Jesus was baptized and came up out of the water, the heavens opened, and the Holy Spirit descended upon Him in the form of a dove. At the same time, a voice from heaven said, "This is my Son, whom I love; with him I am well pleased." This divine affirmation marks the official beginning of Jesus' ministry, identifying Him as the Son of God and publicly affirming His messianic identity.

The baptism of Jesus holds deep theological significance. It represents Jesus' identification with sinners even though He himself was sinless. His baptism symbolizes the sinless Christ taking on the sins of the world and serves as a precursor to His atoning death on the cross. It also prefigures Christian baptism, which would later become a central sacrament in Christianity, symbolizing the believer's identification with the death, burial, and resurrection of Jesus.

The location of the baptism in the Jordan River is symbolic in Jewish history as the river that the Israelites crossed to enter the Promised Land. For Christians, it represents a crossing from the old life of sin to a new life in Christ. Jesus' baptism in the Jordan thus links the Old Testament stories of deliverance to the New Testament promise of salvation through Jesus. The importance of water as an important and significant part of the great ministerial works needs to be correlated to the works for liberation and dignity of mankind in India had to be taken with a pinch of salt.

The Encounter at Jacob's Well

In John chapter 4 of the New Testament, there's a meaningful encounter between Jesus and a Samaritan woman by Jacob's well. This event is significant because it breaks social norms and offers deep spiritual insights through a simple conversation about water.

Jesus, weary from his journey, stops at the well and asks the Samaritan woman for a drink. This request surprises her because Jews typically avoided Samaritans due to longstanding conflicts between the two groups. The conversation quickly shifts from ordinary water to what Jesus describes as "living water." He explains that whoever drinks the water he gives will never thirst again, as it will become a spring of water welling up to eternal life.

The woman, intrigued, asks Jesus for this living water. She is thinking of physical thirst, but Jesus is speaking of spiritual fulfilment. As they talk, Jesus reveals he knows about her personal life, which astonishes her and prompts a deeper discussion about religious truths and worship. Jesus explains that true worshipers will worship the Father in spirit and truth, moving beyond traditional boundaries of place and ethnicity.

This story is profound for several reasons. First, it shows Jesus' willingness to cross social boundaries, engaging with a person whom his society would have seen as an outsider. Second, it shifts from literal to metaphorical, using the concept of water—a basic human need—as a symbol of spiritual nourishment and salvation that Jesus offers to all people, regardless of their background.

Through this encounter, the woman transforms from a skeptical listener to a believer who goes back to her town to share her experience, leading many to believe in Jesus.

The Start of the Social Revolution

Ambedkar's choice to start his social revolution by addressing the issue of access to water was strategic and symbolic. Water, as a basic necessity of life, was something that everyone could understand and relate to. The denial of water based on caste was a clear and undeniable manifestation of inequality and injustice. By challenging this denial, Ambedkar was not only addressing a specific grievance but was also attacking the very foundation of the caste system that supported such practices.

The Mahad Satyagraha in 1927, where Ambedkar led thousands of Dalits to drink water from the public Chavdar tank in Mahad, Maharashtra, was a defining moment in this fight. This act of defiance was a direct challenge to the social norms that had relegated Dalits to a position of inferiority for centuries. It was a bold statement against the inhumanity of untouchability and a call for equality and human rights.

The impact of Ambedkar's actions extended far beyond the immediate context of Mahad. It sparked a broader movement for Dalit rights across India, galvanizing communities to fight for their dignity and place in society. The event also had a significant influence on the discourse around civil rights in India, highlighting the issues of caste and discrimination as central to the struggle for freedom and justice in the country.

Ambedkar's approach combined legal expertise, political strategy, and moral leadership, making him a pivotal figure in the history of social reform in India. His efforts laid the groundwork for future legal and social changes that would continue to challenge caste discrimination. The legacy of his work is evident in the constitutional safeguards against discrimination and the ongoing movements for social equality in India.

Conclusion

The fight for access to drinking water at Mahad was more than just a demand for a basic resource; it was a powerful step in a much larger battle against oppression. It underscored the interconnectedness of social rights and human dignity and highlighted the role of leadership in effecting social change. Dr. B.R. Ambedkar's leadership in this revolution not only changed laws but also transformed how society itself was structured, leaving an indelible mark on the fabric of India's social history.

By starting his social revolution with the claim to drinking water, Ambedkar set in motion a series of changes that would forever alter the landscape of social justice in India, showing that the fight for equality begins with the most basic of human needs.

CHAPTER 5

A Symbolic Rebellion - Burning of Manu-Smriti

Book burning has often been used as a way to control or reject different ideas. It's a serious action usually taken by those in power to get rid of certain books or writings they don't agree with. This practice has a long history and has been seen all over the world.

It has been used as a tool of oppression—aiming to limit freedom of thought and maintain control over cultural and intellectual life.

Romans Acquiring Books from Conquered Territories:

When the Romans conquered new territories, they often took control of the cultural and intellectual treasures of those areas. This was not just to show their dominance but also to assimilate or even erase the cultural identities of the people they conquered. By controlling intellectual resources, such as books and literary works, the Romans aimed to integrate the conquered societies into their empire, often reshaping their cultural landscapes to align with Roman values and norms.

The process typically involved seizing important literary works and either bringing them back to Rome or destroying them if they were seen as a threat to Roman authority or ideology. For instance, during their expansion across Europe, North Africa, and into the Middle East, the Romans would gather books and artifacts that were of historical, religious, or cultural significance. This not only enriched Roman culture but also served as a tool to educate Romans about the new territories under their control.

This strategy was part of a broader Roman approach to governance that saw conquered peoples being gradually Romanized—integrated into the Roman way of life. This included the granting of various levels of citizenship and integrating local elites into the Roman political system, which helped to stabilize and legitimize Roman rule in the eyes of the conquered

The Epic of Gilgamesh and the Library of Ashurbanipal:

The Epic of Gilgamesh, one of the oldest known pieces of literature, was discovered in the ruins of the library of Ashurbanipal in Nineveh. Ashurbanipal, a king of the ancient Assyrian Empire, had collected thousands of clay tablets from across his empire, housing them in his library. This collection included various literary, religious, and scientific texts.

Unfortunately, the Assyrian Empire eventually fell, and the city of Nineveh was destroyed around 612 BC. The library was buried under the ruins, and the clay tablets were forgotten for over two thousand years. It wasn't until the 19th century that archaeologists, including Hormuzd Rassam, rediscovered these tablets during excavations. The tablets had been preserved in the debris of the destroyed city due to extensive fire which was the practice to destroy any conquered territories, which ironically was protected and preserved the clay tablets from further decay or theft.

The rediscovery of these texts provided a wealth of knowledge previously unknown about ancient Mesopotamian culture, religion, and literature. The Epic of Gilgamesh, part of this rediscovery, is a narrative that explores themes such as the nature of heroism, the pursuit of immortality, and the struggle against the inevitability of death. These themes are universal and have resonated through various cultures and eras, providing insight into human nature and the ancient world's view of life and the divine.

In the case of Nineveh, the burning and collapse served to encase and thus save the tablets from being scattered or destroyed by other means over the centuries. This event, though initially a loss, turned into a significant gain for modern historical and literary studies, showing how actions meant to suppress or destroy can sometimes lead to preservation and rediscovery.

Book burning has been used throughout history by various regimes and groups to suppress dissent or control cultural narratives. Here's how some notable instances unfolded:

- **Nazi Germany in the 1930s:** The Nazis conducted large public book burnings. They targeted works by Jewish authors, communists, and others they labeled as "un-German". This was part of a broader effort to cleanse German culture of influences considered harmful to Nazi ideology. The burnings were widely publicized and served as a powerful symbol of the regime's desire to control cultural life and thought in Germany.
- **Soviet Union under Stalin:** Similar to the Nazis, the Soviet regime under Joseph Stalin destroyed books and artworks that conflicted with Stalinist ideology. This was part of a larger effort to centralize control and reinforce the communist doctrine as the sole intellectual authority. Books that promoted capitalist ideas or criticized the communist regime were often destroyed, and authors of such works faced persecution.
- **Qin Dynasty in Ancient China:** The first Emperor of China, Qin Shi Huang, famously ordered the burning of books in 213 BC. His goal was to standardize the thoughts, philosophy, and history of China, aligning them with legalist principles that supported his rule. This act aimed to eliminate intellectual diversity and enforce a single-state ideology.

These instances show that book burning is often a tool used by those in power to limit access to information and reinforce their ideologies. Despite its repeated use throughout history, such actions often highlight the regimes' fear of alternative ideas and their potential to inspire resistance and change.

Why Manusmriti?

The Manusmriti, also known as the Laws of Manu, categorizes society into four main groups called varnas. These groups determine what jobs people can do and who they can socialize with. Here's a simple breakdown:

- **Brahmins:** These are the teachers and priests. They are considered the highest group and are respected for their knowledge and role in religious ceremonies.
- **Kshatriyas:** This group includes warriors and rulers. They protect and govern society.
- **Vaishyas:** These are the traders and farmers who handle business and agriculture.
- **Shudras:** This is the group that does various service jobs. They are placed at the bottom of this social system.

Below all these groups are the Panchamas (the fifth group) or Dalits in recent times, historically known as "untouchables." They are not included in the varna system and often face harsh discrimination and exclusion from mainstream society.

The Manusmriti sets rules that keep these groups separate. For example, it says that Dalits and Shudras should not participate in religious rituals, attend school, or eat food with people from higher varnas. These rules make it difficult for Dalits and Shudras to improve their social status and lead to them being treated unfairly compared to others.

By placing these groups in a fixed system and setting strict rules, the Manusmriti enforces inequality and justifies unfair treatment based on birth. This has a deep and lasting impact on society, making it hard for people to see each other as equals.

Patriarchal Norms

The Manusmriti is known for reinforcing patriarchal norms within society, clearly delineating roles for women that are restrictive and subordinate compared to those of men. Let's delve into the specifics of these norms and understand their implications in more detail:

Role of Women According to Manusmriti

In Manusmriti, women are explicitly placed under the guardianship of men throughout their lives. Starting from their fathers in childhood, to their husbands after marriage, and eventually, if widowed, to their sons. This continuous supervision implies that women are never truly independent or capable of self-governance according to the text. Such prescriptions are not merely advisory but are enforced through social and legal means, deeply affecting the everyday lives of women.

Restrictions on Property and Inheritance

The Manusmriti also imposes severe restrictions on women's economic freedoms. It generally denies women the right to own property independently or claim equal inheritance as their male siblings. This economic dependency ensures that women remain under the control of their male relatives, limiting their ability to exert influence within the family or the wider community.

Legal Inequalities

One of the more striking aspects of Manusmriti's approach to gender roles is its legal bias against women, particularly evident in its handling of marital fidelity. Women accused of adultery face harsh penalties, which could include severe social ostracism and physical punishments, whereas men guilty of similar infractions often receive much lighter sentences. This disparity not only highlights the gender bias in legal terms but also reinforces the notion that women's value and respectability are closely tied to their sexual behavior, much more so than for men.

Societal Impact

The societal impact of the gender norms prescribed by the Manusmriti is profound and multifaceted, affecting various aspects of life and culture in societies where these norms have been influential. Let's explore how these norms shape societal attitudes and the long-term implications for women's status and their participation as equals in society.

Reinforcement of Gender Roles

The Manusmriti establishes specific roles and behaviors that are expected of women, deeply influencing societal expectations and norms. When such roles are legally and culturally codified, they become entrenched in the collective consciousness of society. This codification makes it challenging to change these perceptions over time, as they are seen not just as cultural norms but as moral imperatives. Women are often valued primarily for their adherence to these roles, particularly those related to modesty, fidelity, and subservience.

Limitations on Women's Rights and Freedoms

By restricting legal rights, such as property ownership and inheritance, the Manusmriti effectively limits women's economic independence and mobility. Economically disempowered, women are more dependent on male relatives for financial security and social status, which can restrict their ability to make autonomous decisions. This dependency also impacts women's educational and professional opportunities, as families may prioritize resources for male members whom they view as future breadwinners.

Social and Cultural Stigmatisation

Women who challenge or fail to conform to these prescribed roles may face social and cultural stigmatization. This can include ostracism, which not only affects their mental and emotional health but can also lead to tangible consequences such as reduced support networks and fewer economic opportunities. Such stigmatization reinforces compliance with traditional roles and discourages dissent, keeping the patriarchal structure intact.

Implications for Gender Equality

The entrenched gender norms from Manusmriti make achieving gender equality in society challenging. As long as these ancient prescriptions are revered and followed, the social fabric will inherently support the unequal treatment of women. Efforts to promote gender equality must therefore contend not only with contemporary biases but also with historical and deeply ingrained societal norms that are resistant to change.

The Broader Societal Impact

The influence of the Manusmriti extends beyond individual women, affecting the broader society by maintaining a gendered division of labor and social functions that can hinder comprehensive social and economic development. Societies that enforce rigid gender roles may fail to effectively utilize the talents and potentials of all their members, leading to a loss of diversity in thought and a slowdown in innovation and progress.

Symbolic Burning

When Dr. B.R. Ambedkar burned the Manusmriti in 1927, it was much more than just setting a book on fire. He did this to strongly oppose the unfair social rules that the Manusmriti supported. These rules had been used for a long time to justify treating people differently based on their caste—where they come from in society.

By burning the book, Ambedkar was not just rejecting the old rules written in it. He was also asking for a new way of living where everyone is treated equally and fairly, no matter their background. This act of burning the book was a powerful way to show that he and his followers did not accept discrimination and wanted change toward equality and justice for all.

The Event and Its Witness

The Manusmriti, often seen as a traditional text outlining societal norms, has historically been viewed by some as an authoritative guide on social conduct and structure in India. It outlines a rigid caste system where Dalits or those outside the caste hierarchy often referred to as "untouchables," are placed at the very bottom. This system not only categorized people based on their birth but also dictated their social status, work, and interactions with other castes.

Significance of the Manusmriti in Society

The Manusmriti provided guidelines that were deeply ingrained in social, legal, and religious practices. It justified the social order by assigning roles and duties to different castes, advocating that these roles were ordained by sacred authority. For Dalits, this often meant limited rights, restricted access to resources, and a life of servitude and exclusion from mainstream society.

By burning the Manusmriti, Ambedkar publicly denounced the caste-based discrimination and inequality it perpetuated. This event was executed on 25 Dec 1927 the same day when the world celebrates the birth of Saviour. This dramatic gesture was meant to inspire a movement towards abolishing caste distinctions and promoting equality. It was a call to reject age-old discrimination sanctioned under the guise of tradition and religious authority.

The burning of the Manusmriti by Dr. B.R. Ambedkar was a significant event in the history of social reform in India, and the presence of notable figures like Vinayak Damodar Savarkar highlighted its importance. Savarkar's presence at this event is particularly noteworthy due to his complex views on caste and social policies, adding depth to the act's historical interpretation.

Vinayak Damodar Savarkar, a prominent figure in the Indian freedom movement, is often remembered for his contributions to the development of Hindu nationalist ideology. His views on caste reform were somewhat progressive for his time; he advocated for dismantling certain aspects of the caste system but his approach differed significantly from Ambedkar's. While Ambedkar saw the caste system as inherently oppressive and sought its complete abolition, Savarkar saw potential for reform within its framework.

The presence of Savarkar, who had his own distinct and influential following, at an event led by Ambedkar, a champion of Dalit rights and social justice, signified the broad impact of Ambedkar's actions. It showed that the event was not just a statement within the Dalit community but was a moment of significant political and social importance that drew attention across different spectra of Indian society. This convergence of leaders with differing views underscored the complexity and the widespread relevance of the issue of caste discrimination.

Their presence indicated that the issue was of national importance and merited attention from all sectors of society, including those who might not typically align with Ambedkar's views on caste and social equality.

Unapproved Law: The Manusmriti

The Manusmriti, historically revered by certain upper-caste groups in Hindu society, was seen as a legal and moral code that prescribed and legitimized a rigid hierarchical structure based on caste. While it held a position of authority in some circles, it was far from universally accepted across the diverse social spectrum of India. For the Dalits and other marginalized communities, the Manusmriti symbolized an oppressive framework that institutionalized their inferior status through divine ordinance and ancient tradition. It was not a text that they had accepted but rather one that had been imposed on them.

Approved Law: Community Embrace

In contrast to the top-down imposition represented by the Manusmriti, Dr. Ambedkar advocated for laws and societal norms that were democratically agreed upon and that promoted equality and justice. His philosophy emphasized that laws should arise from the consensus of the people they govern, reflecting the community's values and aspirations, rather than being handed down as unchangeable edicts from a bygone era.

Dr. B.R. Ambedkar's act of burning the Manusmriti in 1927 was a bold stand against the deep-rooted caste discrimination sanctioned by the text. This act went beyond just rejecting a book—it was a public call for change, demanding a shift from old, oppressive laws to new principles of equality and justice.

The Need for New Laws

Ambedkar's action was a demand for laws that everyone in society could agree upon, rather than those imposed by a select part of the community. He was advocating for laws that supported everyone's right to equality and justice—principles that he believed should be the foundation of any society. This was in stark contrast to the Manusmriti, which had rules that most people did not choose or agree with.

Psychological Chains Imposed by the Manusmriti

The Manusmriti, an ancient legal text, significantly shaped the psychological landscape of Hindu society by reinforcing caste-based identities and roles. Its directives were not just rules but served as a framework that defined and legitimized the hierarchical structure of society, deeply affecting how individuals viewed themselves and others.

The Manusmriti delineated clear and rigid boundaries between the castes, prescribing specific duties, behaviors, and interactions for each group. This codification of social roles based on birth contributed to a fixed social order where one's caste heavily influenced personal identity and self-worth. Such a system inherently limited individual aspirations and enforced a sense of predestined limitation among the lower castes, particularly the Dalits.

Identity Formation: The text influenced how people perceived themselves and others, often instilling a sense of inherent superiority or inferiority based purely on birth. This kind of identity formation led to internalized oppression, where individuals from lower castes might accept their societal position as deserved or unchangeable, perpetuating a cycle of psychological subjugation.

Social Order and Compliance: By legitimizing a hierarchical structure, the Manusmriti also fostered compliance with the social order. The fear of social ostracism or even harsher penalties for violating caste norms reinforced the caste identities and limited social mobility, creating a psychological barrier to questioning or challenging the status quo.

Impact on Self-Esteem and Mental Health: The psychological impact of being categorized in a lower caste could lead to lower self-esteem and a host of mental health issues. The stigma associated with caste could affect all aspects of life, including education, employment, and personal relationships, further entrenching feelings of inadequacy and helplessness. The upper caste individuals are no better in this deal, they gain over self esteem so much so to become more cruel than any cruel wild animals.

The Symbolic Burning and Its Psychological Impact

Dr. B.R. Ambedkar's act of burning the Manusmriti was a profound rejection of this psychological bondage. By publicly denouncing the text, Ambedkar aimed to challenge and dismantle the legitimacy of the caste-based discrimination embedded within it. This act was not merely symbolic but catalyzed social change, encouraging those oppressed by these norms to view them as neither immutable nor morally defensible.

Empowerment: The burning symbolized a rejection of imposed limits and was an act of empowerment for many. It encouraged individuals from marginalized communities to question and resist the roles forced upon them by tradition.

Redefining Identity: By challenging Manusmriti's authority, Ambedkar opened the door for redefining one's identity beyond caste-imposed boundaries. This was a step towards enabling individuals to see themselves as equal members of society, deserving of respect and dignity regardless of their birth.

Inspiration for Social Reform: The event inspired further movements and legal reforms that sought to eradicate caste discrimination and promote equality. It played a crucial role in shaping modern India's approach to social justice and equality, influencing policies and the framing of laws that aim to protect all citizens' rights.

By saying no to the Manusmriti, Ambedkar not only spoke out against the injustices of caste discrimination but also encouraged a vision of a society where equality and respect matter most, no matter where you come from. His brave stance still rings true, showing us that making things better often starts with daring to question the way things are and pushing for a society that's fair and equal for everyone.

Conclusion: A Call for Continued Change

This book has shared stories from India's past, focusing on the efforts to fight inequality—stories that are often left out of the main narrative. We've seen how individuals and communities have stood up against unfair treatment, striving for a more just society. Their struggles highlight the deep roots of inequality and the persistent effort needed to uproot them.

Despite the progress made, inequality still exists, affecting many lives today just as it did in the past. The fight for fairness and equality isn't over. It continues every day in small acts of courage and in larger movements that challenge the status quo.

As we move forward, let's remember the lessons from these lesser-known chapters of history. Let's take inspiration from the determination of those who came before us and continue their work. Change is possible when we stand together and keep pushing for what is right.

Our journey through these pages is more than a look back—it's a call to keep working for a future where everyone has the same opportunities to succeed. Let's keep the hope alive and work together for a society where equality is a reality for all.

Creating the land of opportunities where equality, justice and respect for humans are at their best in the world, let my God and all humans born on this land thrive to work it out.

Author Bio

Chinta Srinivasa Rao is the name given by the parents with love reflecting the faith, liking and trends of the day, yet my preference was for the shorter and sweeter version Dr C S Rao adored by Indian Defence Services and loved by my professionals. Born to high school educated parents as a first child of the five children in rural Andhra Pradesh. Faced many life challenges few purely self-made, few handed by family and many handed by society. Evolved into successful medical professional with the help of Constitution of India. Started my career as a young doctor in Indian Army which turned my life significantly with poring luxuries and responsibilities. One fatal event encountered with the poverty stricken Nepali migrant laborers at Indo-China boarder made me to be myself, pushed me towards my purpose of life. This experience steered me towards specialization in Family Medicine at Christian Mission Centers like Christian Fellowship Hospital, Oddanchatram, Tamil Nadu. Furthered my expertise in Clinical Cardiology at Narayana Hrudayalaya, Bangalore, Karnataka. Pursued my Health Management studies getting M.Phil. from BITS-Pilani, Rajasthan. Became legally compatible by pursuing Bachelors in Law (BL) from Nagarjuna University, Guntur, Andhra Pradesh. Presently passionate about combating poverty and distributing equality for the better society with a new concept called COLFE-Compassion on Life For ever and COLFE-CM Compassion On Life For Every Common Man.

"INSTIGATING DIGNITY IN EVERY LIFE" as a vision by eradicating poverty through high-quality, affordable healthcare, achieving this transformative goal within this lifetime.